The Dog

Handbook

Dan Rice, D.V.M.

With Color Photography
Drawings by Michele Earle-Bridges

BARRON'S

Dedication

To my son Chris, and the little black shaggy dog of his youth, Skippy. I enjoyed writing this book immensely and it is dedicated to a pair who also gave me great joy as they grew up together. If there's a doggy heaven, that's where Skip rests.

About the Author

Dan Rice, a veterinarian originally from Colorado, is presently pursuing his lifelong love of writing. *The Dog Handbook* is the tenth book he has written for Barron's. Others include *Bengal Cats, Complete Book of Dog Breeding, Complete Book of Cat Breeding, Akitas, Dogs from A to Z (A Dictionary of Canine Terms), The Well-Mannered Cat, Brittanys, Chesapeake Bay Retrievers,* and *Training Your German Shepherd Dog.* He has also written an anthology of veterinary practice experiences and a children's book. Now retired to Arizona with his wife Marilyn, he keeps in touch with canine research and the fancy through study and writing.

Photo Credits

Norvia Behling: pages vi, vii, ix, x, 11, 12, 15, 17, 22, 26, 33, 39, 40, 41, 44, 57, 60, 61, 64, 66, 68, 70–72, 75 bottom, 78, 81–84, 88, 90, 93, 95, 109, 112, 142, 145; Daniel Johnson: page 75 top; Tara Darling: pages 117–121, 123, 125, 126, 130, 132, 139, 143, 144, 146, 152–155, 157, 159, 161; Kent and Donna Dannen: pages 122, 124, 127–129, 133–138, 141, 151, 156, 160, 163, 164; Pets by Paulette: pages 131, 140, 147–149, 158, 165; Pam Ross: page 150; Judith E. Strom: page 162.

Cover Photos

Front: Kent and Donna Dannen, Tara Darling, Billy Hustace; Back: Tara Darling; Inside covers: Kent and Donna Dannen.

All inquiries should be addressed to:
Barron's Educational Series, Inc.
250 Wireless Boulevard
Hauppauge, New York 11788
http://www.barronseduc.com

International Standard Book No. 0-7641-1152-3

Library of Congress Catalog Card No. 99-23129

Library of Congress Cataloging-in-Publication Data
Rice, Dan, 1933–
    The dog handbook / Dan Rice.
        p. cm.
    Includes bibliographical references (p. 170).
    ISBN 0-7641-1152-3
    1. Dogs. I. Title.
SF427.R4885   1999
636.7—dc21   99-23129
                                                        CIP

Printed in Hong Kong

98765432

Important Note

This pet handbook gives advice to the reader about buying and caring for a new dog. The author and publisher consider it important to point out that the advice given in the book applies to normally developed puppies or adult dogs, obtained from recognized dog breeders or adoption shelters, dogs that have been examined and are in excellent health with good temperament.

Anyone who adopts a grown dog should be aware that the animal has already formed its basic knowledge of human beings and their customs. The new owner should watch the animal carefully, especially its attitude and behavior toward humans. If possible, the new owner should meet the former owners before adopting the dog. If the dog is adopted from a shelter, the new owner should make an effort to obtain information about the dog's background, personality, and peculiarities. Dogs that come from abusive homes or from homes in which they have been treated abnormally may react to handling in an unnatural manner, and may have a tendency to snap or bite. Dogs with this nature should only be adopted by people who have had experience with such dogs.

Caution is further advised in the association of children with dogs, both puppies and adults, and in meeting other dogs, whether on or off lead.

Well-behaved and carefully supervised dogs may cause damage to someone else's property or cause accidents. It is therefore in the owner's interest to be adequately insured against such eventualities, and we strongly urge all dog owners to purchase a liability policy that covers their dog.

Contents

Foreword

A canine companion should share your life, not just go along for the ride. Ownership means more than providing a few doggy necessities and allowing the pet to occupy a small, cleanable portion of your home.

A dog will communicate with you and give as much as you ask for, but you should seek a reciprocal relationship. To share your life with a dog, you must understand its personality, and what your role must be to mold that personality into your lifestyle. If you learn the dog's needs and what brings your companion happiness, you're sure to enjoy the love it gives and blend the dog's life with yours.

Gentleness is understood by both dogs and kids.

It doesn't matter whether your new dog is a purebred or mixed breed, a lapdog or a wolf-cross. Ownership means building a human-canine relationship that teaches the dog to respect your rules of comportment. At the same time, you must learn and respect the dog's idiosyncrasies.

This book is an easy-to-read guide to such a canine relationship. It contains a wealth of ideas and suggestions designed to make ownership of a new dog a pleasant and rewarding experience. Myths are dispelled, theories are expounded, and sufficient information abounds to help you through your new dog's most trying times. Included are:
• a brief account of dog history
• why and how dogs think
• the relationship of wolf instincts to modern dog behavior
• advice on subjects such as selection, what to watch for when searching for the right dog, where to get a dog, and how old it should be
• information relative to bonding and dominance training
• housebreaking and details related to elementary obedience training and Canine Good Citizen certification
• a comprehensive chapter on canine nutrition, with advice on diet,

treats, and foods that are dangerous for dogs

• first aid and emergency procedures including pad wounds, poisoning, bloat, canine cardiac massage, and pulmonary resuscitation

• keeping your new dog healthy: why vaccinations are given, when and why to spay or castrate your dog, and major diseases and health conditions

• pictures and descriptions of 49 popular purebred dogs

Before you read this book thoroughly, I suggest you browse through it. Pick a subject you wish to know more about and, using the index, turn to that page. If I've done my job, you'll find the answer to your query.

This polite Shepherd is waiting instead of scratching at the door.

Preface

My adult life has been blessed by ownership of nine purebred dogs of as many different breeds. Among them were three show dogs, two of which earned their AKC championship. We acquired most of these dogs as adults, their owners being unable to keep them for one reason or another. Their personalities were totally different from one another. We also had the pleasure of sharing our life with one little nondescript mutt.

Our old Schnauzer was no longer playful and our second son, Chris, needed a dog. I took great pains to show him pictures of dozens of different purebreds, hoping to interest him in one. This precocious four-year-old knew exactly what he wanted, and he didn't find it in any dog encyclopedia—Chris insisted he wanted a black, shaggy dog that he would call Skippy.

I'll never forget my first meeting with Skip. A lady came into our clinic early one morning with a box full of tiny, shaggy little puppies she had found, obviously abandoned, huddled in the weeds in the middle of a country road. They were a mile from the nearest house, several miles from town, and their mother was nowhere to be found. Two were brown and black with little splashes of white. One was brown and white, and the other two were jet black, the smallest of which was a female. I immediately knew what to do. I offered to examine and vaccinate the abandoned litter in return for ownership of the shaggy little female. The wise lady knew a good deal when she saw it and gratefully accepted my offer. On my drive home that afternoon, the little black-eyed ball of fur curled up quietly on a towel in a shoebox, in the back of the station wagon.

When I arrived home, Chris ran to greet me, and I asked him to bring me the box from the backseat. He climbed into the car and stared at the tiny shaggy pup—it was love at first sight. He sat petting the wriggling puppy for a few minutes, then he realized that this might be *his* pup. He ran excitedly into the house, holding Skippy next to his cheek and talking to her as she bathed his ear with her busy tongue.

Thus began more than a dozen years of love and devotion. Skip went everywhere the boys went. When her Scottie-like short legs had trouble keeping up with the boys' horses, Chris carried her on the saddle with him. Skip had no bad habits that anyone noticed; she was forever a delight. Trainable, obedient, anxious to please, and almost instantly housebroken, she was never a problem to take camping or fishing.

Devoting most of my life to dogs and their owners, I've learned one thing: There are very few bad dogs but many uninformed or irresponsible owners who bring out the worst in their pets. Dogs aren't cookie-cutter companions. Each is unlike the next with a vastly different personality. Purebreds display temperaments and traits similar but not identical to others of the same breed. Mutts, however, are individuals; most of them are easily trained, exceptional pets. All dogs are malleable and often their personalities and character are mirrors of their families' attitudes. Good dogs are made, not born.

Growing up together teaches respect to both the girl and the puppy.

A laughing Labrador.

Chapter One

Canine Instincts and Traits

Origin of the Dog

According to DNA studies, domestic dogs *(Canis familiaris)* descended from wolves, or dogs share a common origin with wolves. Wolves aren't all alike; neither are their habitats confined to a single locale. Worldwide distribution of wolves of varying types may be associated with the wide variety of present-day domestic canines.

No one can argue the biological similarities of wolves and dogs. They look much alike. Anatomically, they have nearly identical teeth, adapted for seizing, slicing, and tearing. They act similarly; wolves and dogs run in packs when allowed to do so. They have extremely sensitive senses of smell and hearing, and they share the propensity to occupy dens, which they defend.

Dogs' physical appearance (phenotype) is quite malleable, and many characteristics that are visible in the dog but not in the wolf could have been aided by selective breeding of their wolf ancestors. Dogs' eyes are generally rounder than those of wolves. Adult wolves have slitlike eye apertures, but wolf puppies have wider, rounder eyes than their parents do. Dogs' eyelid anatomy therefore could be associated with the selection of parents that retain immature features and a puppylike appearance into adulthood (neoteny). Similarly, dogs generally have shorter muzzles than wolves have, but this might also be the result of selective breeding and neoteny.

Neophobia is an inherent personality characteristic of feral dogs and wolves, and is defined as fear of new environments with new inhabitants. Although dogs exhibit some degree of shyness, or neophobia, through conditioning, that trait is easily repressible.

Domestication

Considering the many jobs we ask our dogs to perform, most of us agree that canines were probably the first species to be domesticated by humans. It's a generally accepted theory that the world's first dogs

Skeletal System

Skeleton—side
1. Nasal bone
2. Frontal bone
3. Auditory bulla
4. Atlas
5. Axis
6. Scapula
7. Thoracic vertebrae
8. Lumbar vertebrae
9. Ilium
10. Sacrum
11. Acetabulum pelvicsocket
12. Pubis
13. Ischium
14. Coccygeal vertebrae
15. Tarsus
16. Metatarsus
17. Phalanges
18. Fibula
19. Tibia
20. Stifle joint
21. Patella (kneecap)
22. Femur
23. Os penis
24. Rib cage
25. Ole canon
    of the Ulna
26. Ulna
27. Metacarpus
28. Carpus
29. Radius
30. Humerus
31. Sternum
32. Mandible

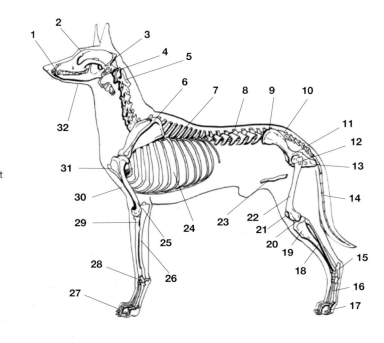

were tamed wolves. Both humans and wolves were predators, occupying a place near the top of their food chains. They had similar appetites and probably fell prey to similar, more powerful predators.

Wolflike carnivores may have followed cave dwellers, scavenging scraps from animals these humans killed. The reverse is also possible—humans may have followed wolf packs and subsisted on the wolves' leavings.

Prehistoric humans had larger, more complex brains than wolves had, probably indicating a greater capacity for knowledge accumulation and abstract reasoning. Recog-

nizing the animal's speed and killing power, these early humans saw the wolf as a potential hunting assistant. They probably employed wolves' attributes to supplement their own food-gathering potential. Wolf puppies were adopted and raised as valuable additions to human families.

Through conditioning, adopted wolf puppies recognized a particular human as the dominant or alpha member of their new family group. To enjoy the benefits of life in this new society they had to submit to human domination. Early dogs that challenged their masters' leadership didn't wind up in an animal shelter or a dog psychologist's waiting room;

they were sacrificed to provide meat for the dinner table and skins for clothes. Thus, a primitive but practical selection eventually produced dogs that were compatible companions and helpers to the people who fed, housed, and kept them.

Prehistoric dog owners discovered other talents of their canine assistants. With their dogs' help, hooved animals were herded and gathered, then, when the need arose, these animals were milked, shorn, or killed for food. Sharing food and shelter with humans, dogs naturally guarded their homes from others, yet another fringe benefit of owning dogs.

Traits of Dogs and Their Ancestors

Domestic canines are loyal to and dependent upon their humans. They literally live for their owners, and they have taken a subservient place in human society. The only reward many dogs seek is a kind word and a pat on the head.

Still, the study of dogs and wolves teaches us many traits that haven't changed much since before they were domesticated.

Instinct

This term means an inborn tendency to behave in a way that is characteristic of a species, a natural and *unlearned* response to a stimulus. It is an innate talent or propensity, and a driving force to act in a certain way.

Pack Action

This term is used to describe the canine instinct to *pack* or join with others of their kind in order to effect greater power and strength. There is an old saying: "One dog is a pet; two dogs make a pack." The pack takes on a character of its own; it is not the sum of the experiences and training of the individuals. Logical reasoning is lost when a pack of dogs forms. This peculiar canine tendency has been long recognized, and a personal experience might amplify dogs' pack attitude.

A gentle, well-mannered Collie that was a child's pet joined company with a Springer Spaniel that was a sportsman's trained hunting dog and a Dalmatian that was also a well-loved family pet. Owners of these innocent-looking dogs lived within a mile of each other in a rural Colorado mountain valley. The dogs were occasionally left outside at night during the summer. This unlikely trio formed their pack several times per month, joining forces to chase sheep, cattle, or horses.

Residents didn't observe these three dogs in a pack, but saw their tracks and immediately concluded that coyotes were chasing and killing the livestock. Ranchers declared war and decimated a fair number of coyotes without benefit to the harassed livestock. Then the truth came out.

One night during a particularly savage attack on a flock of ewes and lambs, the ranch owner shot and killed the Dalmatian that was apparently leading the pack, and seriously wounded the Springer. The Collie escaped injury but was incriminated by his owner, who presented the dog for examination after finding blood saturating the white hair of his head and ruff (sheep blood). These nice pet dogs had been killing lambs and calves, and running horses into fences for several months. Individually, each was a loving family pet. By instinct, none were coursing breeds, and none were vicious.

Pack action of canines is instinctive, and there is nothing we can do about it except provide our dogs with the security they need. Fences, pens, and even the less desirable tie-ups will control their innate desire to pack. Herding dogs, such as Collies, rarely will leave their homes to roam, but under pack conditions, instinct drives them to do so.

Marking

Another instinctive trait of wolves and dogs is to *scent mark*. This innate behavior is stronger in male canines, but is seen in both sexes. Dogs mark their dens and territory with urine or with the oily scent from glands of their cheeks, anal regions, and feet. When a dog raises his hind leg and squirts a few drops of urine onto a fire hydrant, he is marking. This too is a trait we can't stop in our dogs.

Body Language

Postural display is yet another characteristic of canines, both wild and domesticated:

• When meeting a strange dog or man, nonsocialized dogs raise their *hackles* (hair on their backs and necks). This is most easily seen in shorthaired dogs, and it makes them look larger than they are. It is meant to intimidate their enemies and is a good bluff. Sometimes, hackle raising is combined with pulling back their lips to show big, sharp canine teeth that are held slightly apart, ready to snap. Small terriers have mastered this practice; a bristling Scottie's formidable canines will cause all but the foolhardy to back away from a confrontation.

• Ear and tail positions are among the many postural displays by which an observant student can tell what the dog is thinking. For instance, most dogs will tuck their tails between their legs when submitting to a greater power. Likewise, their ears will fall, and the overall picture is that of a smaller dog, one slightly crouched in subjugation.

• Rolling over on the back is the final instinctive submissive action of a dog that is allowing discretion to take control. Its superiors will seldom attack a dog whose tender abdomen is left unprotected.

• The top dog will usually assume another meaningful body posture. Standing tall on stiff legs, the superior dog will strut around the weaker one, perhaps accenting this posture with occasional growls and snarls.

• Kneeling, or placing the forelegs on the ground and lowering the forequarters, is an invitation to play, and is seen in young wolves as well as domesticated canines. Coupled with a wagging tail, this is a display of friendliness.

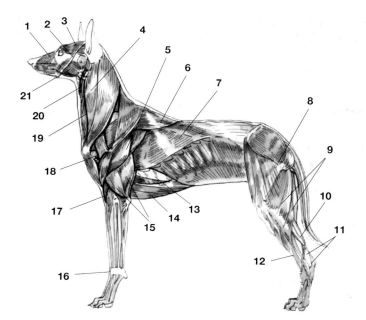

Muscles—side
1. Maxillaris
2. Zygomaticus
3. Scutularis
4. Mastoideus
5. Deltoid
6. Trapezius
7. Latissimus
8. Gluteus maximus
9. Biceps
10. Gastrocnemius
11. Achilles tendon
12. Greater saphenous vein
13. Intercostals
14. Pectoralis major
15. Triceps
16. Carpal sheath or annular ligament
17. Brachialis
18. Acromion deltoid
19. Jugular vein
20. Sterno hyoideus
21. Masseter

• Pulling the lips back over tightly clenched teeth is known as smiling. Interestingly, this facial expression seems to be reserved for humans. Smiling is an inherent trait that is more common in some breeds than others.

• Turning in circles before lying down is another instinctive habit seen in many dogs. Experts say this circling is a holdover from the days when dogs turned around and around to pack down grasses to make a comfortable bed. Others say that since the dog always has its nose to the ground during the rotation, the habit is more likely associated with checking the ground for the scent of its enemies.

• Another less visible inborn trait is digging. Dogs occasionally dig dens under porches and in their runs or yards. For many years, terriers would dig to pursue their quarry underground, and this too is an inherited behavior.

• In many dog breeds, chasing is instinctive; anything that runs will be chased, even if the dog has no intention of killing and eating the running animal. A bad habit? No, just another instinctive trait.

• Gathering gazelles into a tight group was once a means of increasing the kill potential of a group of wolves. In the absence of such animals, many dogs herd children and pets together. This is not a particularly undesirable trait.

• Attacking small rodents is an innate hunting trait stemming from the time when these little animals were the dog's main source of food.

These instinctive traits are so ingrained that they cannot be stopped or modified totally, no matter how much effort is expended.

Olfactory Sense

Scenting or sniffing the wind is another habit long established by wolves and other wild canines. This obviously serves a dual purpose: to discover the scent of prey, and to distinguish predators in the area.

Some breeds of dogs have more acute scenting proclivity than others, probably because olfactory capacity has been used as a major criterion for selective breeding. It is a well-known fact that some individuals within a breed have greater scenting talents than others of the same breed.

Domestic canines have 40 times more olfactory cells than humans have. Newspapers carry reports of dogs locating humans who have been buried by tons of snow or the smoldering rubble left after explosions.

Scenting ability goes unused by many dogs. Some pooches aren't particularly interested in scent trails and are content to fine-tune their scenting ability to detect special odors coming from the kitchen. Even the laziest male dogs have been known to pick up the scent of a female in heat as far away as two miles, yet these same dogs have no apparent interest in following other scents. No doubt, the reason some dogs lack a scenting ability is that they have no need for it; they don't follow scents of prey since their food comes from a bag or can.

Sense of Hearing

Dogs' discriminating auditory sense is another reason for early teaming of human and canine. The wolflike erect ears can hear the slightest sound and are excellent early warning devices. Able to distinguish the sounds of different cars in the distance, house dogs often announce the arrival of their masters even before they can be seen.

Sight

Dogs have highly developed visual capability. Their field of vision is different and in some ways inferior to that of humans, but for their purposes, it is quite adequate. Sighthounds have developed the ability to see quarry from a distance but often have trouble following it up close.

Thinking and Reasoning

Dogs' instinctive actions and personalities are influenced by heredity, but innate habits can hardly explain all of their conduct, nor are dogs' behaviors simply the sum of instincts plus conditioning. Like other intelligent mammals, they are the products of genetics, *experience*, and training.

More than 100 years ago, a dog trainer made a remarkably true statement, one that dog lovers should imprint on their minds: "The common belief seems to be that the dog acts from the impulse of *instinct* throughout its life. Many people concede no higher mentality to the dog than what comes from instinct, and this too notwithstanding that true instincts are independent of experience; while the *dog's knowledge is dependent on experience and education. . . .*" B. Waters, *Fetch and Carry*, 1895. (Italics added for emphasis.)

Dogs have an excellent memory, which gives them the ability to learn quickly by experience. Unfortunately, their experiences are not limited to positive ones; they watch other dogs and mimic their actions. In addition to a great memory and learning ability, your dog has the capacity to think, reason, plan, and act on its plans. It has reasoning powers with which to solve problems. It is a cunning and intelligent animal with a complex mind.

Dogs, like wolves, reason to solve problems. Packs of wolves choose the very young or the very old prey as the most desirable victims; they isolate debilitated or wounded quarry. Reserving the energies of older pack members until younger wolves have tired their prey, the older, more experienced wolves enter the chase, using their knowledge and power to effect the kill.

Similar rationale is noted in bird dogs when they somehow reason that wounded birds will run; therefore, they should pick up the injured ones before they seek those killed by the shot.

Reasoning ability is seen when dogs act heroically. Without prior training or experience they dive in and rescue babies from lakes and ponds. Guide dogs, by means of their analytical abilities, refuse to take their blind charges into dangerous situations.

Human Helpmates

After dogs were domesticated and firmly established as human companions, it was only natural to select the specific types of dogs most desired. Dogs of different sizes, with different talents and personalities, were purposefully bred to serve the needs and fancy of humans. Over the centuries, selective breeding of the best dog for the job brought about the variety of dogs we now see. Dogs have become loyal accomplices to virtually every human endeavor.

Specialization

Some giant breeds were propagated for stamina and strength to carry out alpine rescues. In the North, sled dogs were bred for fleetness and athletic ability. In warmer environs, fleet sighthounds were developed to outrun and kill game, and heavy scenthounds were bred to follow game trails for miles. Dogs were developed to guard property, herd sheep, and to sit quietly on laps.

Sporting breeds' instincts were refined to locate and set upland birds and to retrieve ducks, geese, and other waterfowl. Sportsmen and commercial hunters used dogs in various ways to maximize the effectiveness of hunting with nets, guns, and falcons.

Internal Organs

1. Nasal cavity
2. Sinus cavities
3. Brain
4. Palate (soft)
5. Spinal cord
6. Esophagus
7. Lungs
8. Diaphragm
9. Kidney
10. Ureter
11. Descending colon
12. Trachea
13. Thymus
14. Heart
15. Liver
16. Stomach
17. Spleen
18. Small intestine
19. Urinary bladder

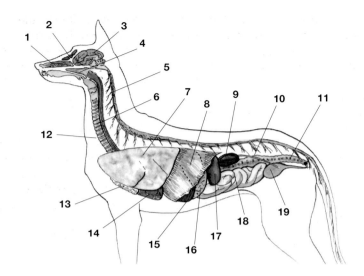

Stewardship

Owners historically have treasured their dogs. They were instruments that made life more productive. Dogs added to human enjoyment and helped fill leisure time. In the past, dogs were often luxuries, adding a note of opulence to their owner's society.

There was a time when only rich sportsmen could afford to keep bird dogs or coursing hounds for occasional hunting forays. Wealthy dynastic lords of the Orient bred tiny "sleeve dogs" to warm their beds and adorn their personages. Other decorative and diminutive dogs were found scampering about queens' chambers. Distinctive dogs were bred specifically to run beneath dignitaries' coaches, and huge mastiffs were developed to guard castles along the Rhine. These specialized dogs weren't found in the homes of the masses.

In some instances, dogs were essential to agriculture and industry, and were recognized as such. In the seventh century a folk law assessed heavy fines for anyone who killed a herdsman's dog.

In 1494 Petrus de Crescentis, a Greek instructor of agriculture, stated, in the book *Field and Furrow Cultivation*: " . . . shepherds shall take right good care of their dogs . . ." In another place he added: "Our daily needs lays it upon us that we must first have good (dog) trackers that they may hunt up the wolves and track them." He continued: "The manor house and property should be guarded by large and mighty dogs that are a terror to thieves and other knaves," and commented: "Owners should make their dogs comfortable nests, and they must train them with patience." These venerable statements teach us some important lessons: A dog's value has long been recognized—and *patience* is more than a virtue; it's a necessity.

Dogs were fewer in number and safer in those days. Overbreeding wasn't a problem and dog pounds were rare. Dogs were protected, abuse was uncommon, and canine husbandry was carefully practiced. Then came human affluence, and with it the desire to own dogs. As more families began to collect dogs, their value was depreciated. Today, dog overpopulation has skyrocketed. Every breed and mixed breed are found in shelters and pounds. Millions of these unwanted dogs are destroyed every year in the United States.

To treat "man's best friend" with indifference and neglect is a crime, an offense to our culture. Their usefulness hasn't diminished in the past few centuries, but their perceived value has sunk to the level of other disposable products. Dogs are often purchased on whims and dumped when they are no longer wanted.

Chapter Two
Selecting Your New Dog

Are You Ready for a Dog?

There are many reasons for sharing your life with a dog; however, wanting a dog to love is a small part of dog ownership. If you truly love dogs, you will want the dog to be happy in your home. In order to be a good dog owner, you must make a sincere, thoughtful commitment. Before you buy, consider what kind of companion you will be, *not* what kind of puppy you should get. *Try to match your desires to the needs of the dog.*

Obligation and Dedication

Acquiring a pet on impulse often ends in disaster. Dogs make very poor birthday or Christmas presents. Owning a dog for any reason requires a long-term commitment that deserves careful thought by its owners. The new dog will share your home and heart for many years, and the decision to obtain it should be discussed with, and clearly understood by, all household members.

Before you shop for a new dog, consider a few aspects of dog ownership.

Time

Be sure you have time to spend with a pet. Unfortunately, this item is frequently overlooked, especially if there are young children in the family and little Bobby needs a companion. Grown-ups often mistakenly delegate a dog's care to a four- or five-year-old child. That's unfair to both the child and the pet.

Do you have time to train a dog? Training isn't another job to do; it's relaxation and enjoyment, but most of all, it's an obligation that must fit into your daily schedule. It requires no particular talent; anyone of average intelligence can do it, but if you can't spare the *time*, if the hours spent in training, play, and walks won't mesh with your current obligations, maybe you should rethink obtaining a new dog.

Necessary Facilities

Do you have sufficient physical space for a dog? For an outdoor dog, at least a fenced yard and a warm, dry doghouse are needed. Perhaps you will want a kennel and enclosed run to house your dog at certain times. Are these facilities within your pet budget?

If the dog is destined to share your home, do you have an area of the yard or some other place to dedicate as a toilet area during and after the housebreaking period? Do you have a spare room or a bathroom in which to confine the dog while housebreaking? Do you object to cleaning up after a dog? Can you handle a puppy crying at night and the inconvenience of getting up to put the pup outside and bring it in again?

Are you frequently away from home? Have you investigated boarding kennels? How much do they charge? Do you have reliable friends who will care for your new dog when you are away?

Monetary Considerations

Can you financially afford a dog? Purchase price is only the beginning of dog ownership; there are routine health and insurance fees to consider. Every dog, even under the best circumstances, will occasionally require veterinary assistance. Call a veterinarian to obtain an estimate of the average cost of annual vaccinations and parasite prevention.

Your dog will deserve the best food. What will it cost to feed it each year? Regular yard treatment may be needed to help protect your dog from ticks and fleas. Consider the cost of

Which one should I choose?

dishes, beds, collars, leashes, toys, and chewies.

Can you afford specialized training? If you plan to enter your dog in competitions, have you calculated the cost of a professional trainer, training classes, equipment, and possibly a handler's fees? Are you willing to spend the money for training aids?

Patience

Dog ownership is a labor of love, but it takes great patience and determination. Be honest—a hot, quick temper that flares frequently isn't compatible with dog ownership, so proceed no further before rethinking the project and talking to dog owners.

Training

Will you teach the dog yourself? At the very least, you must give your dog some home schooling. He must be taught good manners or he will be a liability rather than an asset.

Necessary training includes house-breaking, good manners, collar and leash training, and some fundamental obedience work. A trained dog is a joy to behold, and an untrained, unresponsive pooch is an albatross necklace. Without training, your dog will be worse than a nuisance; he will be an embarrassment to your household.

Timing

In order to get a new dog started correctly, everyone in the family must be ready. Don't bring your pup home immediately before the holidays or his needs might be lost among new toys. Perhaps it would be best to purchase dog accessories and a picture of the pup to place under the Christmas tree, then bring the puppy home after the holiday is over and the family has settled into its normal routine.

Dogs make poor surprise Christmas or birthday presents.

If you plan to take a vacation during the first few weeks of July, don't bring your new dog home in May or June. In order to train the dog, you must be home; you can't delegate this responsibility to a friend or boarding kennel. Consistency is the key to housebreaking and leash training, and it is better not to interrupt this training while you are on vacation.

Puppy or Adult?

Whether you want a puppy or an adult depends on economics, the age of children in the household, the amount of time you can devote to housebreaking and training, and other items covered below.

Adult

Often, what you see is what you get; adults have reached their maximum size, coloration, and coat type. Their personality is fixed, although many learned behavioral attitudes can be altered.

Adult dogs are sometimes more stable than puppies, depending on their previous family experiences. Introducing an older dog to a new environment can be traumatic. Adjustment to a new family and new rules and personalities is likely to take longer with mature dogs. Getting to know a grown dog will take weeks instead of days, and a lengthy get-acquainted and bonding time is usually required. During this time you will need to observe the dog's bad habits and plan and initiate a corrective or reeducation program.

Consider the following:

• Adult dogs will probably be vaccinated, although they may need boosters.

• Spaying or neutering may have been done, which will diminish your expense.

• You can easily arrange outside housing for an adult outdoor dog as you have a good idea what type of fencing you will need, the size of the doghouse you will need, and the dimensions of a kennel run.

• If you are considering an inside dog, be aware that adults are often housebroken and may already have acceptable house manners.

• Eating habits are usually established, but they may need changing to suit your lifestyle.

• Usually, dogs of six months or older have been introduced to collars and leashes, and some may even have had a bit of obedience training. The old saying related to old dogs and new tricks is easily disproved. With patience, dogs that are several years old *can* be taught new habits and new rules, and often these lessons are quickly absorbed and mastered. The attention span is longer in an adult, and more advanced training can be initiated.

However, there is another consideration: Bad habits die slowly. If you acquire a grown dog with unacceptable behavior, you may spend a great deal of time and effort changing this conduct. For this reason, it's best to take an older dog into your home only if you are able to return it, if necessary.

Puppy

Owning an eight-week-old puppy is an adventure. Cuddling him, watching him clumsily play, and being with him during the first few nights away from his mama are events nearly everyone should experience. A puppy usually bonds to his first owner quickly and easily. Within a few days he will follow you around, getting underfoot and rarely roaming more than a few yards from your presence; however, consider the following:

• Petting and wrestling with a pup is great fun for the children of the family, but great care must be taken to be sure the pup doesn't get the worst of these encounters. Puppy bones break easily, and puppy character is formed by the early treatment they receive. Children and pups alike must be carefully monitored when together.

• Housebreaking time is particularly tedious and exasperating for the uninitiated. You will spend days or sometimes weeks running to and from the toilet area of the yard, often in the middle of the night. You must meticulously clean up messes in order to avoid future accidents caused by the odors of past mistakes.

• Puppies are subject to diseases and prone to mischief not usually associated with adult dogs. Pups, and sometimes older dogs, must be checked periodically for worms. The pup will need vaccinations and boosters, and you will need to change the pup's diet as he matures.

• You must puppy-proof your home to accommodate the youthful, sharp-toothed little furniture chewer. Spaying or neutering represent additional expenses of puppy ownership.

Veterinarians' Opinions

When choosing your new dog, consider more than the outward appearance of the pet. Consult with knowledgeable people to learn about personalities; try to match what you want with what the particular dog has to offer. Talk with a veterinarian about your choice of a purebred or mixed breed dog. In all probability, those professionals have had experience with similar types of dogs and will be able to provide insights on your selection. Veterinarians' opinions are invaluable as they handle many different dogs every day and have first-hand knowledge of the idiosyncrasies and qualities of particular types or breeds.

In addition to having the pup examined, you can get an idea of the specific aspects of proper dog care in your locality. Risks of certain diseases indigenous to your region may be brought to your attention. Hereditary faults prevailing in your chosen breed can be outlined, and you may receive advice on how to deal with these and other problems.

Purebred or Mixed Breed?

What you want from a dog usually determines whether you are in the market for a purebred or a mixed breed dog. The advantages of purebred animals are consistency of appearance, size, coat type, and color. Personalities and other mental traits of purebreds can also be better predicted than can those of mixed breeds. When you acquire a Cocker Spaniel, you can be sure it will mature to a certain size; it will be similar to other Cockers in appearance. Its coat, ears, nose color, eye color, and temperament will be similar to other Cockers.

Mixed breed puppies may mature to look like their dam, their sire (if known), or neither. Their coats may be smooth, wiry, rough, or somewhere in between. Adult sizes are difficult to ascertain, as are their expressions. These variations are multiplied when either or both parents are from mixed backgrounds. Surprises and lack of predictability are associated with the large gene pool from which the mutt pups emerge.

Purebred dogs generally have more genetic faults and deformities than do mixed breeds. Mixed breeds usually have a certain amount of *hybrid vigor* (heterosis), which, under some circumstances, result in stronger and more disease-resistant dogs. A mixed breed pup is likely to have a very individual personality, seemingly unrelated to either of its parents.

The temperaments of mixed breeds are often quieter and more stable than those of purebreds, although this characteristic is not consistent. Temperament is partially genetic and partly the result of experience and training. Many purebreds have a notably quiet temperament, and an occasional mixed breed is unpredictable.

Before you select a purebred or a mixed breed, decide what you expect of the dog. If you have a desire to exhibit it in conformation shows, obedience trials, field trials, herding tests, or other AKC-sponsored events, you must start out with a purebred.

If you want a companion, a family pet, or a child's dog and have no aspirations of winning blue ribbons,

a mixed breed should fill your need nicely. Mixed breed pups and adults are plentiful, both from shelters and private homes. They cost less to buy, and may be easier to handle. Mixed breed dogs can compete in Frisbee contests, 4-H obedience, and non-AKC agility trials, and are included in the AKC-sponsored Canine Good Citizen program (see page 74).

Male or Female?

There is very little difference between the sexes when looking for a pet or companion that will be neutered at or before puberty. If you choose a female, the cost of spaying might be greater than the cost of castration of a male, but when pro-rated over the life of the dog, cost is a minor consideration. Both sexes can be trained with a similar degree of success. There is no appreciable difference between males and females in terms of health care costs, provided your pup is spayed or castrated.

If you are considering entering your purebred puppy in conformation show classes or field trials, it can't be neutered, and you must remember that females come in heat for about three weeks, twice a year. That equates to six weeks lost from each year if you are entered in showing or training classes. You can enjoy AKC tracking, obedience, and agility competition with a neutered purebred dog.

Some of us appreciate the temperament of females; others prefer masculine characteristics. Do you have other male dogs in the household? If so, a new male may present an aggression problem unless they are raised together from puppyhood or are neutered; however, neutering won't necessarily stop male aggression and pack-oriented domination. Females are usually more gentle than males, but this too is relative and varies with individuals.

If you are buying a female dog and don't plan to have her spayed before she comes into heat, you'll need to board her while she is in season to prevent unwanted puppies. This is an added expense to be figured into the cost of keeping an unspayed dog.

If you plan to show your purebred dog, do you also plan to raise puppies? If so, a show-quality female is your obvious choice. Few males are good enough to be considered stud dogs, and even if you have a male that wins his share of ribbons, he isn't likely to be in great demand for breeding. Show-quality bitches are usually quite expensive to purchase, and that's only the beginning of costs associated with breeding and raising quality puppies.

Age

From birth to seven weeks, your new pup is continuously learning the latest rules of nest etiquette, what is and is not acceptable conduct according to Mom. During this period, the puppy receives hands-on experience in socializing with siblings. It's a serious mistake to remove a pup from this environment before he has completed the course in how to get along with other dogs.

For this reason, most breeders keep puppies until they are at least seven weeks old. Try to bring the pup home as soon as possible after that age. The critical socialization and bonding period between pups and humans extends from shortly after birth to about three months of age. Pups should be introduced to gentle human handling as early as possible. During the post-weaning period, your new dog will quickly learn to trust his human family, a trust he will honor throughout his life.

Pups are often housebroken and have learned acceptable manners by eight to ten weeks of age. This period is also the time when bad habits may be learned and those too are firmly imprinted in puppy minds.

If, for some reason, you can't bring your pup home before it is three months old, select a pup that has been frequently handled by the breeder's family. A dog that matures without human companionship, and has only other dogs with which to relate, may be slow to bond with a human family. Such a dog may require extensive handling and conditioning to become a good companion. However, most dogs will bond at any age with an attentive family if given enough love and attention.

Temperament and Disposition

It's often difficult to identify personality differences among puppies in a litter. Temperament is critical when choosing a pup, and you should consider it carefully.

The dam and sire will often furnish a general idea of what their offspring's attitude will be like when grown. Shy dogs aren't good companions, or, at best, they are more difficult to train and handle. Stay away from puppies whose sire or dam is timid, quarrelsome, or belligerent.

Choose a happy pup, one that comes quickly to you and wants to follow you when you leave. Beware of snappy, timid, or shy puppies. The most aggressive pup is less desirable than one that is more laid back. Mischievous playing is not an undesirable characteristic, but a pup that is forever attacking his siblings is not likely to be an easily trained companion.

The Right Breeder

Purebred dog breeders may be located in a number of ways. Contact the AKC for the name of the current national or regional club secretary. Ask for a list of breed club members in your locality. The AKC has a web page that may be accessed to find Breed Club Secretaries and other information; it is listed under Useful Addresses and Literature, page 169.

To meet purebred dog fanciers, go to a dog show in your region. Attend obedience trials, herding tests, agility contests, tracking trials, Frisbee contests, or field trials where you can meet other fanciers of those specific endeavors. Various dog magazines usually carry advertisements for purebred pups. Information about shows and trials may be obtained from the *AKC Gazette*, a monthly publication of the AKC (see Useful Addresses and Literature, page 169). This publication also contains a breed listing with many kennels' advertisements.

There are good and bad purebred dog breeders, just as there are good and bad pet shops. The number of litters raised each year doesn't equate to the breeders' expertise or knowledge. Choose a breeder with a good reputation among his or her peers, and one who has produced winning dogs. Look at the accomplishments of the dogs in the kennel as well as the puppies' housing.

Purebred Cost

A purebred puppy naturally costs more than a mixed breed since it must conform to certain standards. Does the cost reflect the dog's worth to you? If you have visions of distinction or recognition for your new puppy, a purebred is the right avenue to take to acquire ribbons and trophies—if the dog is good enough.

If you want to participate in AKC-sanctioned events, such as field trials, retriever tests, herding trials, or obedience trials, you must begin with a purebred dog. A high-quality dog obtained from a legitimate breeder will have a fairly high price tag, and rightly so. This is an area where you will probably get just what you pay for. Bargain basement purebreds can be heartbreakers!

Newspaper Ads

If you seek a purebred dog through ads in your local newspaper you may find trouble instead. Legitimate breeders occasionally advertise in newspapers, but ads are often placed by backyard breeders who aren't interested in the betterment of the breed. Neighborhood litters offer a questionable source of purebred dogs, but before you buy a backyard breeder's pup, be sure to examine the AKC registration and pedigree of the dam and sire. If the puppies aren't yet registered, or if their parents are less than two years old, beware—these puppies are often less expensive than breeding kennel-raised dogs, and may prove to be fine pets, but it is unlikely you will receive health or performance guarantees of any kind. It is equally implausible to find a show-quality animal from a backyard breeder.

Puppy Mills

Worse yet, newspaper ads may promote pups from "puppy mills," establishments that maintain bitches of various breeds, and whelp hundreds of pups each year. They are notorious for mass-producing poor-quality pups of questionable health and heritage. It is usually quite easy to spot a puppy factory. When you arrive, a litter may be presented without the dam. If you ask to see her, an excuse is usually made, or if you see her, she may be in pitiful nutritional condition. If you gain admittance to the kennel, you will usually see various breeds in crowded, dirty conditions with very little provision for exercise, and thin, overworked dams. Pups from these puppy mills should be avoided at all costs!

Pet Shops

Pet shops may be a viable option for you. Shops very seldom have the dam or sire of a purebred pup, and rarely can you see the puppy's siblings; however, many pet shops maintain pedigrees and complete records of their puppies' origins, and

you may learn the name of the kennel that raised the pup and thus satisfy your requirements. If the pup is AKC-registered, a pedigree can be obtained from that organization, but not usually before purchase.

Mixed Breed Pups

Although they cost less, mixed heritage pups are just as susceptible to various contagious diseases as purebreds. The same selection precautions should be exercised when obtaining a mixed breed as would be practiced when buying an expensive purebred.

Mixed breed pups, affectionately referred to as mutts or mongrels, are often found through ads in the local papers. They are sometimes marketed via a shopping cart in front of a supermarket. Some find their way into pet shop windows, and often they are sold from cardboard boxes in front of their dam's homes. They are usually the result of a family pet escaping from the yard while in heat. She runs down the street and returns a few hours later with a twinkle in her eye. Two months later, nondescript puppies arrive. Many of these pups will become excellent

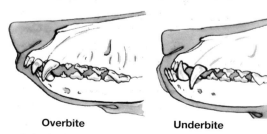

Overbite   **Underbite**

Overshot and undershot jaws are serious show faults but rarely cause problems.

pets and wonderful companions. If healthy, the mutt is often quite intelligent, eager to please, easily trained, and quick to learn tricks.

Besides their looks, there are other differences between mixed breed pups and purebreds. These cute little mutts will rarely have received their initial vaccinations, and they usually are given away at an earlier age than purebreds are. If you decide on a mixed puppy, don't take it from its dam before it is six or seven weeks old.

Is the purveyor of a mixed pup entitled to any monetary recompense? The litter is truly the fault of the owners for not providing more security for their female, but you shouldn't object to paying a nominal fee for a strong, healthy pup. The owners of the dam should be compensated a small amount for feeding her during her pregnancy and prior to weaning her litter. They are also entitled to some consideration for the food the puppies have consumed. Mixed puppies raised in a household with children probably have received as much or more handling and socialization than purebreds. Ask if the money received from puppy sales will go toward the cost of spaying the dam; such a program deserves your support.

Crossbreds

Sometimes a purebred bitch is mated with a purebred of another breed. If this crossbreeding is done with sufficient attention to the size and build of each parent, as well as the trainability and personality, the offspring may prove to be excellent companions. In recent years, more crossbreeding has been done and many lovely crossbred pups are the result. At the risk of being ostracized by the AKC and purebred clubs all over the world, I can think of several instances when crossbred pups might be quite desirable.

Some guide dog institutions are experimenting with crossbreds in their breeding and training programs with some success in improving or stabilizing temperament, conformation, and trainability. Time will tell how this experiment goes.

When a very delicate purebred toy male is crossed with a sturdier purebred female of another toy breed, the progeny are often hardier and stronger. These crossbreds are frequently in high demand, and many are great pets.

Many hunters purposely cross their purebred pointers with bird dogs of another complimentary breed to gain some heterosis, or hybrid vigor. This has been done for many years with mixed, but often favorable, results. Sometimes the unfortunate gunners find the progeny of such breeding have inherited the worst characteristics of both breeds.

Consider the Parents

In purebreds, your pup is a reflection of his parents. If both have done well in shows, tracking, or obedience, a likelihood of similar talents exists for their offspring. If only the dam is present, ask to see a picture of the sire, and, if possible, pictures of his other progeny. Don't rule out a litter because of the dam's physical condition alone. A good dam produces so much milk for her puppies that she is nutritionally drained after about six weeks of nursing and she may look a bit rundown. She may have a saggy abdomen, be thinner than normal, and in poor coat when you see her, but she should be clean, active, friendly, and inquisitive. Look at her puppies from previous litters, if any are available.

Selecting a Healthy Pup

If you're simply looking for a healthy companion dog, and have no interest in formal obedience or show competition, your selection will be easier. To assure that your pup is in good health, look it over from stem to stern before you buy it.

When confronted by a litter of happy little face lickers, it's difficult but important to concentrate on health issues. Even a novice can inspect a pup and make a rough evaluation of his health and personality. When you observe pups at weaning age you won't be able to see every fault they possess, but you'll make a more intelligent choice if you follow these guidelines.

Remember this if you forget everything else: *It is impossible to pick a robust pup from a puny litter.* If you see an assortment of skinny, runny-eyed, lethargic, coughing puppies, stand back! Don't make the mistake of taking a sick pup home with the guarantee that it will get better in a day or two. Don't buy a puppy receiving medication. Wait until the course of therapy has been completed and a veterinarian has pronounced the pup healthy.

Look at the puppies' surroundings. If there are dirty food dishes lying about, overturned water bowls, and other signs of poor sanitation, beware! If the pups are confined to a yard, look for piles of feces and uneaten food attracting flies. Don't adopt a pup from an unhealthy environment because you feel sorry for it.

Picking the Best Pup

When you approach a litter, be careful not to frighten the pups. Remember your height: You tower above the tiny pups, and your size alone is sufficient to cause apprehension in them. When you enter the room or yard where the puppies are housed, stand back and observe the litter from a few feet away:
• Make a mental note of those pups that don't join in the tumbling and play. Perhaps one or two will run and hide behind their dam or nesting box. Those pups are often insecure or poorly socialized, and are probably too young and inexperienced to leave the nest environment. Visit the litter more than once if all the pups seem timid; a few days at this age will make a big difference.

This one likes me.

the sound came from, then goes to investigate the can. Such a pup might be an excellent choice. Puppies that flee instantly when a new sound is heard may not be good companions.

• Select an inquisitive, affectionate puppy, but one that doesn't aggressively attack its siblings. A pup with a domineering or aggressive attitude when playing with its littermates isn't the best choice.

• Be cautious about adopting a hyperactive puppy, one that never seems to tire. This trait is often indicative of a hard-to-train pup.

• You should reject a pup that immediately takes a defensive stance when you reach for it. If it snaps, screams, or otherwise seems frightened, it's probably not the pup for you. It may grow out of this attitude with time and socialization, but you should not burden yourself with such a trait.

• Concentrate on pups that are anxious to meet you rather than those hanging back. If a pup is curious about the visitors, but doesn't show any particular fear of them, put a plus beside that pup's number. If a puppy with many or all of the above-described desirable qualities tries to follow you when you leave, your selection is made.

The Final Test: As mentioned, it's important to make yourself as small as possible when you first approach a puppy. Lying down on the floor or lawn (if practical) is an excellent posture to take. Don't grab him as he runs by, and don't corner

• Sit or kneel down when interacting with the litter. Wad up a piece of paper, toss it across the floor, away from the puppies, and watch their reaction. If a pup watches you toss the paper wad, chases it, and brings it to you, your selection is probably made.

• Put a few marbles or pennies in a soda can, shake it behind your back to get the pup's attention, then roll it across the floor. It's a good sign of the pup's confidence when it twists its ears, looks around to see where him. If the family has handled the pups, and if you were careful in your evaluation of the litter, he will catch you; you won't have to chase him.

Take him into another room or away from the rest of the litter. Sitting on the floor, watch his attitude when you place him beside you. If he climbs onto your lap and one end is wagging and the other is licking your face, you're nearing a good selection. Gently cradle him in your arms in an upside-down position and scratch his tummy and chin. He should allow this attention with little objection and without immediately squirming to turn himself right side up.

Congenital Faults

With your pup standing or sitting on your lap, feel his abdomen for evidence of an umbilical hernia, which may be identified as a soft protrusion of tissue under the skin, about the size of a marble, at the site of his navel. In a seven- or eight-week-old puppy, hernias are soft; when they are pressed they may disappear into the abdomen. Hernias are easily repaired, but they require surgery and represent an additional expense to you.

If selecting a male, check for the presence of testicles. They should be descended into his scrotum by eight or ten weeks of age; if not, they may never descend. This defect doesn't present a serious problem in a companion animal or an obedience dog, but if you plan to enter your new dog in show competition, leave the pup with the breeder until the testicles descend into place, or pick another pup.

If you are choosing a mixed breed, be aware that undescended testicles should be surgically removed when the pup is mature. This surgery represents yet another expense that you should consider.

Health Records

You've found the perfect puppy—a bundle of energy at playtime and an affectionate little sweetheart when picked up. There are a number of documents that should accompany your new puppy. Among them are records of when and by whom the pup was vaccinated, the product used, and when other vaccinations are due.

The date a worm check was done and the results of that fecal exam should be included, together with the date of treatment for parasites if the fecal exam was positive. Health papers should specify what product was administered, and the date.

Records should include the dates of health examinations, and the name and address of the veterinarian who performed the exams. If your new dog was seen for an illness, it should be specified, as well as the name and dosage of medication used.

If heartworm, tick, or flea preventive medication has been started, the dates and the product used should be noted.

The pup's diet should be recorded, including the quantity, brand name, and frequency of feeding.

What Documents Should Accompany Your New Dog

- AKC registration papers if purebred
- Pedigree if purebred
- Date of birth
- Breeder's contract
- Diet being fed, both specific brand and times per day
- *Veterinarian's health report:*
  - Statement of health when examined
  - Date examined
  - Date of first vaccination
  - Date of booster vaccinations, if any
  - Date and results of last fecal exam
  - Recommendation for next vaccination
  - Recommendation for next examination
  - Date of previous illness and treatment for same

The breeder of your new dog should have this information readily available, and usually more; be sure it's in writing. Continued preventive health care depends on complete health records.

AKC Papers

If the pup's parents are AKC-registered, you should receive a puppy registration document at the time you take your puppy home.

A pedigree is a record of several generations of the puppy's ancestors. It has no particular value in pet-quality pups, but is very significant if you have purchased a show or competition dog or if you intend to breed it. A pedigree is no better than its source and many are written by breeders and other nonofficial sources. A certified pedigree is available from the AKC for a fee if you furnish the pup's registration number.

Any special considerations that apply to the purchase should be put in writing. If you agree to spay or castrate the pup by a certain age, write it down. If the breeder guarantees the puppy to be in good health, get that in writing as well, together with the duration of the guarantee. Purebred dog breeders will often replace a pup if your veterinarian discovers a disease or deformity present at the time of purchase. Be sure the terms of the guarantee clearly specify whether it assures you of your money back, or a replacement pup.

Chapter Three

Getting Acquainted with Your Dog

Daisy and Dandy

In various chapters throughout this book, the hero is named either "Daisy" or "Dandy." This technique is designed to eliminate any sexism and to circumvent the use of the clumsy terminology *he or she*. Also, by naming our dog, use of the neutral pronoun "it" is eliminated; after all, this book is about your new dog, a real personality, not an *it*.

Bonding

Bonding is the term used to describe the progressive trust relationship between dog and master, regardless of the dog's age. It begins the day Dandy arrives in your home and never ends. Each time you call him to you, he responds, and you reward him with petting, praise, and sometimes a tidbit. He will bond with every member of your family and perhaps with some friends, providing those people also treat him with trust and love.

Dandy's strongest bond is with the person with whom he spends the most time, the one who takes him for walks, plays with him, and teaches him manners. If it is your desire to train him, you must strengthen the bond between you daily. Calling his name frequently is one way to tighten the bond, as is your praise when he responds. Never let your temper flare, and always play by the same rules; be consistent with Dandy's treatment.

Puppy Bonding

Birth to three months is the most important time for a puppy to establish a lifelong bond with his master. If you handled Dandy before he opened his eyes, he will remember your scent, and bonding will begin at that point. If you handle him frequently while he is still in the nest with his dam and siblings, the bond between you will be even stronger.

If you obtain him at the usual time a puppy leaves the nest, he will be about seven weeks old. Bonding begins immediately upon arriving in

your home. If his experiences with you are positive, gentle, and frequent, the bond strengthens.

It's easy to bond with a pup. Each time you pick Dandy up for a quick cuddle, he learns to trust you more. Every time you feed him, play with him, or take him for a walk, he appreciates you and your attention and the bond between you is reinforced. If you've obtained a lapdog, he will surely like being held, and will depend on you to give him creature comforts every day. His dependence upon you is exactly what you want.

There is more about the bonding phenomenon in this book in the sections on housebreaking and other training.

Adult Bonding

Bonding with an adult dog that has been raised by someone else is a greater challenge. Often, the dog will be bonded to another individual, and you must substitute yourself for that person. The worst-case scenario is seen when the adult dog hasn't bonded to anyone with a steadfast trust.

The bonding procedure is the same as with a puppy, but the process usually takes much longer. Often, you won't know the dog's name, and that slows the bonding. In the case of an adult dog with many bad habits, or one with a grouchy disposition, establishing a trust relationship is sometimes nearly impossible.

Don't rush the process. Teach Dandy his new name first; say his name every time you see him. Call him to you frequently for a tidbit or an ear scratch. Begin short but regular sessions of petting and grooming. Feed him small meals frequently from your hand, repeating his name and petting him while feeding him.

The dog's acceptance of your kindness and gentleness is the beginning. When he routinely comes to you for food and grooming, put a collar and leash on him and take him for walks in your backyard. Make every walk a pleasant experience for him. Don't scold or physically correct him for any mistakes he makes at this stage.

Test him to see if he enjoys a game of catch or fetch. If he responds to either of these games, play them with him daily. If he becomes belligerent or possessive with either game, put the toy away until later. Don't give the dog any reason to compete with you. This means no tug-of-war, or roughhousing.

Once he begins to show evidence of bonding with you, proceed with dominance training as described later (page 60). Don't attempt to begin obedience training until you are sure Dandy accepts you as the alpha dog in his pack. Bonding with an adult dog often starts slowly, but sometimes the dog will display a sudden change of attitude and will become quite possessive of his new master.

Handling a Puppy

Tiny puppies don't break easily, but when small children and weaning puppies are left together unsupervised, it often leads to problems. If your family has toddlers or children who have never been around young animals, they should be taught that Dandy is a playmate, not a toy.

We ignore children who drag about stuffed animal toys by their tails or ears. We laugh when they playfully toss a teddy bear across the room, or poke at the eyes of a stuffed dog. You must protect your new dog from similar fates, and teach children to respect and handle the puppy carefully.

If your new dog is grown, children and adult members of your family must take particular care. An older dog of any breed needs to become accustomed to his new family at his own pace. Rushing the relationship is dangerous. If you press him, you may provoke timidity or shyness, if not defensive aggressiveness. Have patience; establish a trusting bond between your family and the dog before you handle him excessively.

Picking Up and Holding a Pup

Dandy's mother picked him up by the scruff of the neck, or sometimes placed his head in her mouth to carry him. That was when he was much smaller and lighter. You should never lift him by the forelegs, but rather, kneel down, slide one palm under his chest, and the other under his belly, and gather him up. Support the pup's rear end with one hand and the forequarters with the other.

Most tiny pups can be carried by an adult human in one hand if the arm is slid under the pup's body, with the hand supporting the pup's chest. The weight of the pup is cradled on the forearm, and the fingers lightly grip the pup's front legs.

Teach children to pick up and carry Dandy with both hands. They should hold him in their arms,

Kennels and runs are nice to confine dogs when you can't be with them.

cradling him snugly to their bodies, and taking care not to squeeze him too tightly. When they release him, they should kneel down and place him gently on the floor. Never drop him—a fall of even a foot can cause serious injury to a young pup.

Dog Furniture

Everyone needs a few personal items they can call their very own. This includes Dandy, the newest member of your family. Whether he shares your home or lives in the yard, you must provide comfortable accommodations for him.

Outdoor Facilities

If Dandy is to live in the yard, be sure he has suitable quarters, including a warm doghouse that is preferably located within the confines of a strong kennel fence. His

house might be of the igloo variety, or a more conventional molded fiberglass type. If you have tools and talent, you can construct the doghouse from wood. In any case, be sure to plan ahead. Design the doghouse to fit Dandy when he's grown. Keep the doghouse door as small as possible to reduce drafts, and place it toward one end rather than in the center of the doghouse. A raised threshold, several inches above the floor, will also help to stop breezes in the winter. If Dandy will be living outdoors in all types of weather, his home should be snug, leak-proof, and only inches taller than his head.

To avoid cold and dampness, the doghouse should be placed on a pallet or porch that elevates its floor a few inches above the ground. Place some type of warm bedding in the house. Straw or wood shavings provide good insulation from the cold, but some dogs develop allergies to those materials. Old blankets or a piece of foam make good beds, but if they get wet, they're difficult to dry out. When the weather is inclement, check the bedding daily, and change it when damp.

If you live in a cold climate, position the doghouse behind a windbreak and under a lean-to roof to protect its door from blowing snow or rain. If you live in a hot climate, the lean-to roof will shade the dog's home.

The Run

If Dandy is to be left alone for several hours, it's best to build a chain-link run surrounding his dog-house. This run should be firmly anchored to the ground to inhibit digging, and the fence should be tall enough to prevent him from jumping out. This may vary from 4 to 6 feet (1.5 to 2 m) tall, depending on his adult size.

This run isn't a place to keep Dandy confined continuously; it should be a place where you are sure he will remain safely for a limited period of time. It should be located in an easily cleaned corner of the yard, where drainage is good. Ideally, the area where it is built will slope at least several inches from front to back, so there won't be puddles of rainwater at the front of the run where he will spend most of his time.

The surface of the run should be clean sand or soil, never sharp gravel. Concrete-floored runs are easier to clean, but they often cause pad abrasions.

Pans and Dishes

Perhaps you will elect to feed Dandy by the free-choice method. In that case, you'll need to obtain a hopper type of feeder, one that will hold a couple of days' ration. It's never a good idea to put more dry dog food in the hopper than will be consumed in two days. The feeder should be kept where you can see it easily, to assure that Dandy has sufficient food for the day, and to be sure it hasn't been contaminated with trash, flies, or other bugs. If your home has a porch, this is the ideal place for a feeder, or you may place it next to his doghouse when he is to be confined to his run for a day.

Stainless steel dishes used to feed canned food should be washed daily, and Dandy's stainless steel water dish should also be cleaned thoroughly every day. If possible, place his dishes in a dishwasher to ensure their cleanliness.

The use of plastic dishes isn't advised for food or water as they often succumb to his sharp teeth, and he may swallow a bit of the plastic. Some plastics can deteriorate in time when constantly exposed to water or food, adding their chemicals to his diet.

Ceramic or glass food and water bowls can be broken, and if ceramics are poorly fired, or contain lead glazes, various toxins may emanate from them and contaminate the dog's food and water.

When purchasing the stainless steel bowls, consider buying a rack to prevent them from being pushed around while Dandy is eating. The rack can be fastened to the porch floor and will assure that the bowls will stay where you put them.

Collars

Dandy will need at least two collars. The first should be a flat, nylon or leather buckle-type collar with a nameplate firmly fastened to it. This nameplate should carry his name and your name, address, and phone number. Even if he is identified by tattoo or microchip implantation (see page 36), he should wear this visible

Dog Facilities and Equipment Needed

- Fenced, dog-proof yard
- Safe and secure run, if outdoor dog
- Doghouse, platform, and shade
- Bed for indoor or outdoor dog
- Stainless steel dishes for food and water
- Crate or wire pen
- Chewies and safe toys
- Web collar, training collar
- Short and long leashes
- Grooming equipment
- Identification tag
- City or county license

identification. The flat collar will be his everyday uniform. He should be trained to wear it as soon as he arrives in your home, and he should wear it virtually all the time.

You should purchase a special training collar when Dandy's schooling begins. Often called a *choke* collar, it may be made of nylon cord or chain. More is said about choke collars in the section on training, beginning on page 59.

Except in rare instances, don't use a prong collar. Prong collars are devices sometimes used by trainers to handle difficult or obstinate dogs and should never be used by the average dog owner. They can easily be abused and may cause irreparable physical and mental damage to the dog.

Leashes

If Dandy is a pup, a lightweight nylon leash about 4 feet (1.2 m) long will suffice for the time being. If he is an adult, buy a 6-foot (2-m) stronger nylon web lead. Another type of lead that is quite handy, depending on Dandy's age, is a retractable nylon leash, which is available in various lengths and strengths. The retractable lead is not used for training, but it serves well when Dandy has absorbed rudimentary obedience knowledge.

Purchase a 20-foot (6.1-m) length of strong, lightweight nylon line to use for training. It should be attached to a snap on the collar and will be used when teaching the *come* or *recall* command (see page 67), and other disciplines.

Bed

Bedding used in outdoor doghouses has already been discussed. If Dandy is allowed in your home, furnish him another bed of some type. It need be nothing more than an old blanket, folded several times, or it may be a wicker basket, depending on his size, and your taste. Dog beds of all colors, shapes, and sizes are available in pet supply stores. If you wish, Dandy can be trained to sleep in his crate.

Crate

A dog crate or kennel should be furnished for all indoor dogs, regardless of their size or age. This crate will be used when housebreaking, and can be used in many other ways, as you will learn in the training section. The crate should be large enough to fit Dandy as an adult. It might be a molded fiberglass traveling kennel, or in some cases, a portable wire pen or cage.

While Dandy is still a puppy, the kennel serves as his refuge, and an adult dog uses the crate as his den.

House Dog

Just as an outdoor dog needs a doghouse and run, the indoor dog must have some equipment as well. Puppies tire of being constantly carried about. They are ambitious creatures but they need rest away from their human family. Before you turn your pup loose in the house unattended, there are some points you should consider.

Puppy-proofing Your Home

Is your house ready for Dandy? Puppies are mischievous and can be rather destructive little creatures. Before leaving him alone in your home for more than a few minutes, you should do a quick hazard inventory. Items generally considered safe for the family may be dangerous for a new puppy. Look around for some of the following puppy hazards:

• Telephone or computer cords make wonderful tug-of-war toys for a pup. Be sure Dandy can't reach them. Appliance and lamp cords are particularly dangerous. If plugged in, chewing can cause mouth burns or fatal electrical shock. Unplugged cords that are attached to irons, toasters, radios, and other appliances may be tugged with disastrous results.

Puppies love to destroy houseplants.

• Chemicals such as oven cleaner, drain chemicals, pesticides, and other poisonous household products should be stored out of Dandy's reach. Laundry soap, bleach, dishwashing soap, silver cleaner, and other such products, often kept under the kitchen sink, present a grave danger to curious puppies. Plastic pot scrubbers and steel wool as well as sponges may be chewed up and swallowed and can require surgical removal.

• If Dandy gets into a cupboard, try to ascertain what objects or chemicals may have been swallowed, read the labels, contact your veterinarian, and watch the pup carefully for signs of illness such as lethargy, vomiting, or diarrhea.

• Houseplants are also attractive targets for puppy attacks. Potted plants can't fight back and usually die. A mixture of damp potting soil, leaf shreds, stems, and roots are messy when spread over the carpet, but more important, a few common houseplants and garden plants are poisonous and can cause serious illnesses in dogs. Silk flower arrangements or artificial foliage are not usually poisonous but they may upset Dandy's stomach, resulting in vomiting and diarrhea.

• Rooms filled with children's treasures are a wonderland of dangerous dog toys. Foam rubber balls, plastic toys, seashells, dolls, and other gimcracks and gewgaws threaten your new dog. A small sponge-rubber jacks ball may look harmless enough, but Dandy may swallow it, and unless it is retrieved quickly, it can require surgical removal. It's best to keep doors to kids' rooms closed and off-limits to the pup.

• Bookshelves appear as a potpourri of leather and paper toys.

• Curtains or blinds swinging at Dandy's eye level may be attacked without provocation.

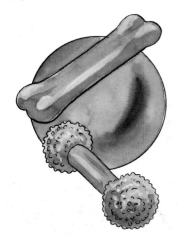

Safe dog treats.

• Tablecloths and coffee-table scarves, hanging innocently over the edges, are irresistible targets for a new pup.

• Tasseled throw rugs provide great entertainment for a mischievous pup.

Infant gates are inexpensive and easily installed to close off a room or two for Dandy. A portable dog pen can be moved from room to room and will serve the same purpose. These pens are available from any pet supply store and are much less expensive than the valuables they protect. Crating the pup is another way to control his actions when you can't watch him.

Outdoor Dog

If the decision has been made to keep Dandy outside and a doghouse is provided in your fenced backyard, you're all set to turn him loose, right? Better think again.

Fence Construction and Height

Obviously a backyard fence should be tall enough to prevent Dandy from jumping over. Don't make the mistake of assuming that a short fence, which is fine when Dandy is a pup, will continue to do the job when he's grown up. Consider the adult size of your new dog when you order fencing materials, and remember that athletic dogs require taller fences than dogs with more sedentary natures.

A fenced yard is a perfect place for a pup or an adult dog, but when Dandy gets bored, thoughts of escape may drive him to chew on a wooden fence. If the fence isn't properly anchored or doesn't extend into the ground several inches, he may decide to dig out.

Outdoor Dangers

• Chemicals that have been recently applied to the lawn or garden should be watered well into the soil to prevent Dandy from contaminating his feet, then licking the toxins off. When watering the lawn after chemical application, be sure not to allow Dandy to drink from pools or puddles. Keep him off your treated lawn for 48 hours.

• Garden hoses can be punctured if they are not hung out of reach of the venturesome Dandy, and in the garden shed are a number of other hazards that threaten your new dog. Fertilizers and insecticides present major threats to dogs. Dandy may chew on a bag, box, or sprayer hose, and ingest toxic chemicals.

The danger of each chemical product is plainly stated on its label. If there is a possibility Dandy has consumed any garden chemical, call your veterinarian immediately and provide the label ingredients and the amount consumed, if it can be ascertained. Don't attempt to treat the animal on your own unless you are unable to reach a professional, then read the package label for instructions. A small puppy has a rapid metabolic rate that makes the

Boredom makes dogs want to escape.

danger even greater and the need to get immediate professional help more demanding.

• If Dandy has access to the garage, keep the floor and driveway clean and free from engine fluids that may drip from your car. Windshield washer fluid and other alcohol-containing products are equally dangerous.

• Antifreeze may contain a kidney toxin that can kill your dog. It has a

Drinking antifreeze is often fatal.

Household chemicals pose dangers to puppies.

over an open can and step in the caustic chemical. If that happens, immediately rinse his feet and legs with gallons of cool water. Then wash them with soap and water and call your veterinarian. Keep paint, turpentine, thinner, and acetone well out of the dog's reach.

• Backyard swimming pools are often equipped with escape ladders constructed for two-legged swimmers. If you have a pool, provide a means of escape for your dog even if he is not invited to use the pool.

All puppies are subject to mischievous activities that land them in trouble once in a while. By identifying hazards ahead of time, you might save your puppy's life.

sweet taste that dogs like, and, unfortunately, treatment is not very effective even when the poisoning is discovered early. If antifreeze poisoning is suspected, waste no time in obtaining professional help.

• In your workshop, there are more dangers. Paint removers are particularly dangerous; even a quick investigative lick can cause severe tongue burns. A clumsy puppy might tip

Introducing Family

Upon arrival in your home, Dandy should be allowed to investigate his new quarters. If he is a weanling puppy, this usually doesn't take more than a few minutes; an older dog might take a week. One of the most difficult jobs you will encounter is keeping your hands off the new dog, but it is important that he acclimate to his new surroundings before he is handled.

Once he is accustomed to his home, yard, and toilet area, you can introduce him to your family. In the case of a young puppy, this is easily and quickly accomplished. Position the children and other adults on the lawn or carpet, and allow the pup to go from one to another. Licking the

Garden chemicals are dangerous for dogs.

muzzle of his siblings, parents, and other dogs in his nest environment was a method of greeting. In his extended nest, it is still his way of becoming a member of the pack. It is a natural subservient action. Some experts warn against allowing a pup to lick his family's faces and arms, but I've never known of any diseases being transmitted in that manner.

If no one grabs him, picks him up, or otherwise deters his rounds, he will accept the entire family without a problem. It is important for every member of his new pack to pet him, speak his name in low tones, and praise him.

After the introductions are made, Dandy should be allowed to frisk about and play with the children of all ages. Warn family members not to allow him to mouth or chew on them or their clothes. When he does this, don't scold the pup, simply turn and walk away, paying no further attention to him.

Other Dogs in the Home

For the safety of the pup, start the new relationship with the older dog on a leash. Dandy will instinctively assume a submissive posture when he is introduced to his older canine roommate. He may turn over on his back, and, once sniffed and pawed by the older dog, he will hop around, licking the older dog's face, trying to initiate a game of tag.

Each time he meets the older dog, he will display less humility, and will eventually be accepted by the other dog. If the older dog is jealous, be sure to give equal attention to both dogs.

Children

Most children would never purposefully injure a puppy, but neighborhood children sometimes present a problem. If they've never been around a puppy, they may try to roughhouse with Dandy, hurting or frightening him. Don't take chances. Be present when neighbors come to play, and if the activity gets overly ambitious, take Dandy into the house and crate him. This is especially important if he is tiny. If he's a larger pup, he might snap at a child who pulls his tail or grabs his ear. Puppy teeth are needle sharp and can cause serious damage to a child's face or extremity.

Other Pets

Don't make the mistake of leaving Dandy unsupervised in the same room with another pet, whether smaller or larger. His instincts may cause him to grab and injure a kitten, parakeet, hamster, gerbil, or other small pet. He may antagonize and be bitten by an older cat or a pet ferret or turtle.

Established pets of the household should be introduced to Dandy in stages. Monitor them closely the first few times they are together. If there is any indication of fear on the part of one pet, or aggressiveness on the part of another, keep them separated. Generally, a puppy and a kitten or cat will reach an agreement within a few minutes. Be sure to trim the front claws of your tabby before she is introduced to Dandy, and soon they will usually curl up together.

New Dog Socialization

Social means having to do with human beings living together as a group in which their dealings with each other affect their common welfare. *Socialization* means conformity to group living, adjustment, or adaptation to the common needs of this human social group.

Therefore, new dog socialization means how well or to what degree a dog has adapted to his human environment, how he fits in, how happy he is, how he has accepted his role in human society. Virtually everything we have discussed previously is important to socialization. The way a new dog is handled, the time he is given to adjust, and his ability to find his niche in the family without undue pressure are all parts of his socialization.

If a puppy is treated well, never abused, and properly trained, he will socialize easily. This process usually moves along at a rapid pace when the rules are rigid and unchanging. You should set objectives and goals for every phase of Dandy's socialization. If these aren't being met in a timely manner, consider why. Are you too impatient? Are your goals realistic, considering the age of your

puppy? Have you spent the necessary time bonding, training, and playing with Dandy? Have you displayed a consistent attitude?

An older dog may socialize quickly or not, depending on his previous experiences. Dogs are intelligent, thinking individuals. Their knowledge is a combination of their inherited instincts and their cumulative experiences. If Dandy is a year old or more, and was well socialized in another family with similar values, and if you set comparable rules to those of his previous home, there should be no problem. However, if he was taught no manners and didn't know what was acceptable behavior in a human household, you can expect to have problems.

Kindness and consistency are the keys to solving all canine socialization problems, regardless of the age of the dog when you acquire him. If you treat the dog gently, using a soft voice, never allowing an argument to begin, he will respect you. That respect will lead to trust, and trust will bring socialization. If you display a bad temper, strike the dog, or are inconsistent with your demands, he will never trust you. More is said about socialization in the training section.

Identification

We mentioned nametags earlier; while those visible means of identification are important, they can be removed or lost.

Tattoos

To permanently identify Dandy as your dog, make an appointment with your veterinarian to tattoo his ear or abdomen. With your social security number or some other set of numbers and letters permanently written on his body, you will be able to identify and claim him under all circumstances. The presence of such identification will deter thieves who might steal him.

The tattoo should be registered with a national organization that maintains a log of identification numbers matched with your name and address. The cost of this registration is minimal and may reunite you and your companion if you should ever be separated.

Microchips

Permanent identification is also possible by implantation of a microchip under Dandy's skin. The problem with microchips is they can't be seen and must be found with a scanner. This means that, in order to be identified, Dandy must be in a pound, shelter, or veterinarian's office where a scanner is available.

While there is no doubt about the value of microchip identification, you might consider a tattoo in addition to the chip.

Tags

The time-honored identification is a dog tag. The best type is a stainless steel tag, one that is riveted securely to Dandy's everyday collar. These tags have the advantage of being readable by anyone, anywhere. Most dogs that disappear aren't stolen; they have simply wandered off or followed other dogs to seek adventure or mischief. No matter how well trained Dandy is, or how secure your yard fence might be, the possibility of a gate being left open does exist. Usually, your dog will remain in his neighborhood, and if wearing a collar and tag, he will be returned or you will be called before he ventures into a roadway or street. Even if he is picked up by the dog warden, you will be contacted quickly, and the fine you are charged will be less expensive than a veterinarian's fee for treatment of car accident injuries.

Chapter Four
Routine Dog Care

The Coat

Dandy's coat quality is a reflection of his nutritional status and general condition. To maintain a beautiful coat requires more than brushing or combing it once in a while. If he is maintained on a premium dog food and is exercised often, his coat will probably always look great. Nutritional considerations are discussed in the following chapter.

Internal parasites rob the dog of nutrition, and are thus associated with dietary insufficiencies and a poor coat. External parasites such as fleas or lice rob the dog of nutrition regardless of its diet.

As Dandy ages, his ability to absorb certain nutrients is impaired; his nutritional needs change and if those needs aren't met, he may display coat problems. Parasitic infestation and old dog health are discussed in the Diseases and Illnesses chapter, page 92.

Taking proper care of your new dog includes regular grooming. Like people, every dog thrives on good grooming; it's a vital part of preventive health care.

Trimming

Some dogs, notably poodles, have long, curly coats. If Dandy is one of the breeds (or mixed breeds) with a coat type that requires regular clipping or trimming, you have two choices: You can buy the necessary equipment and learn to clip his coat yourself, or you can pay a dog groomer to do it for you.

If you decide to groom him yourself, invest in good clippers and enroll in a class in grooming. There is more to making a poodle look like a poodle than you might think. Cockers, some terriers, and other long-coated mixed breed dogs should be clipped regularly as well. The cost of a grooming class and a pair of good clippers will be made up many times over in your dog's life.

Combing and Brushing

A comb will remove dead hair and mats from your dog's coat. This is important to prevent hot spots, which are areas of moist dermatitis or topical skin infections. Removal of mats will uncover other skin irritations, diseases, and parasite infestations as well.

Even short and medium-length coats require some combing and brushing. Your investment in quality stainless steel combs is recommended. If Dandy has a slick coat, like that of a Dalmatian, a slicker brush or grooming mitt is the only equipment needed. A grooming mitt is a cotton glove or mitten with a special rubber or soft plastic palm that is covered with flexible nipples. The mitt fits on your hand, and the dead hair is removed as you pet the dog with it.

If he has a rough coat like a Scottie or Westie, purchase both a comb and brush. If he is long-coated like an Irish Setter or Afghan, you will need a couple of combs as well as a good pair of scissors with which to cut out mats. Scissors or mat splitters should also be part of your grooming equipment for silky-coated dogs like Yorkshire Terriers.

Plucking or hand-stripping is done with the fingers, taking a few hairs at a time. Dandie Dinmont Terriers, West Highland White Terriers, Lakeland Terriers, and several other breeds that are professionally groomed for conformation shows should be plucked to remove excess hair. By hand-stripping, the coat is thinned, but not sculptured. This technique is difficult for most owners to perform and should probably be left to breeders or professional dog show groomers.

Technique

In addition to the proper equipment and grooming classes for some

Grooming should begin right away.

Grooming Equipment Needed
- Combs, both regular and flea
- Brush, rubber curry comb, or grooming mitt if the dog is short-haired
- Canine toothbrush and special toothpaste for dogs
- Blunt scissors
- Mat splitter if the dog is long-haired
- Nail trimmer
- Styptic stick
- Cotton balls for ear cleaning
- Rubbing alcohol or witch hazel for ear cleaning
- Dog shampoo without insecticides
- Old towels
- Hand-held hair dryer
- Shampoo hose for tub faucet

ing. If you see any redness or excessive matter, or if he is squinting, check him later in the day. If the problem persists, call your veterinarian, or make an appointment to have Dandy examined. Don't use human eyedrops in his eyes unless his problem is properly diagnosed and the veterinarian recommends their use. The problem could be a grass seed or other foreign object caught under his eyelid, or it might be a superficial scratch on his cornea. The wrong medication might be detrimental to recovery.

breeds, you need time and patience. Grooming your dog isn't a chore, and shouldn't be treated as such. It should be done on a regular basis, in a specified manner. It need not take hours to accomplish, and if you find yourself spending that much time, you might rethink the process.

Start as soon as possible, preferably when Dandy is a pup. Place him on a table from which he shouldn't be allowed to escape, hold him still, and spend three to five minutes with him. If you will groom him every day while he's still a puppy, you'll find it easier to accomplish weekly grooming sessions when he is grown.

Eyes

Grooming isn't limited to brushing Dandy's coat. You should check his eyes for signs of irritation or matter-

Ears

Dandy's ears should be wiped out with cotton balls, either dry or slightly moistened with rubbing alcohol or witch hazel. If you find excessive wax in his ear canals, clean them as thoroughly as possible with a cotton ball and your finger. If the ear seems tender or painful to your touch, or if he holds his head tipped to one side, make an appointment with your veterinarian. The problem might be ear mites or a grass seed that has become lodged in the ear canal.

Teeth

Dandy's teeth should be checked and brushed at least weekly, preferably more often. Dental hygiene is another bit of preventive medicine that can be easily accomplished if begun while Dandy is a pup. Your investment in a canine toothbrush and paste will pay for itself many times over.

Nails

Dogs that dig or exercise on concrete or asphalt sometimes never need their front nails cut, but their hind nails may not wear off.

You should be able to trim Dandy's nails without help. Like many other procedures, it requires proper equipment and some training to be efficiently performed, but it is something you should do regularly. Have your veterinarian show you the proper way to clip your new dog's nails.

If you wish to try it yourself, buy a pair of well-made scissors-type nail cutters. Trim Dandy's nails regularly, cutting only the tips off, being sure not to cut into the *quick* or vascular part of the nail. If trimming produces a drop of blood, don't worry; simply hold a styptic shaving stick against the cut nail for a couple of minutes and the bleeding will stop. Keep Dandy quiet for an hour after such an accident, preferably in his crate, where any blood seepage can't stain your carpet.

Bathing

This is a part of grooming that generally should not be done on a regular basis. Except for poodles

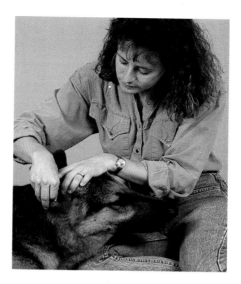

Correct method of cleaning ears.

and other breeds or mixed breeds that require frequent clipping, dogs need bathing only once or twice a year, at the time of their seasonal shedding. An exception is when Dandy's coat becomes filthy or stained and esthetically demands cleaning.

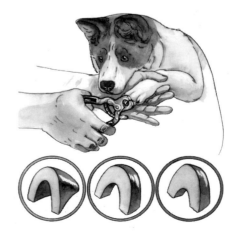

Take care not to trim nails too short.

41

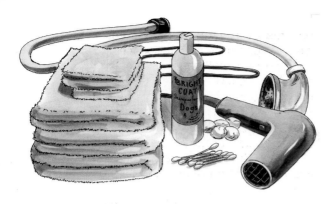

Tools for bath time.

has a heavy coat, use a handheld hair dryer on the warm setting. If the weather is warm and dry, he can be allowed to go outside and shake, but be aware that most dogs love to roll on the lawn immediately after a bath.

Exercise

Another important part of your new dog's care is exercise. Although you have provided Dandy with a run, and he has access to a big back yard, that is not usually enough.

When

Big yards provide dogs the opportunity for exercise, but by himself, he has no incentive to run about. Puppies usually get plenty of exercise while they are young and have children with whom they can play. In the average household, the novelty of a new dog rapidly wears off and the thrill of romping with a new puppy soon diminishes. Remember the commitment you made before you acquired a dog!

Why

Dogs of all sizes and ages require regular exercise. As pups, it helps them develop strong muscles, bones, and joints. As young adults, it strengthens and maintains their bodies. As old dogs, exercise keeps their minds alert, and helps to provide happiness in their declining years. Exercise is important in order to maintain shiny coats at all ages. Dog's digestion is improved and proper body weight is easier to

When wet, mats tighten and become nearly impossible to clear, so it's best to comb the coat free of mats before bathing. When that has been done, place Dandy in the bathtub, and, with a hose attached to the warm water faucet, soak the coat by holding the hose against his body, minimizing splash. When the dog is thoroughly wet, shut off the water and apply a mild dog shampoo (one without insecticides), working it well into the coat. Shield his face, keeping the soap from reaching his eyes and ears. When he is thoroughly lathered, rinse the soap from his body, using the hose attachment held against his body and keeping the water away from his face.

If you have no shampoo hose on your bathtub or shower, invest in one with a rubber attachment that can be easily removed when not in use.

When Dandy is well rinsed, towel him dry, rubbing briskly. If he has a fine coat, use a cream coat conditioner to make combing easier. If he maintain when regular exercise is provided.

Probably the least appreciated but most important aspect of regular exercise is bonding with your dog. Dog writers often extol the virtues of bonding with a new puppy but neglect to say that bonding isn't limited to age or condition of either the dog or the human. As you exercise and play with Dandy, he focuses on you and develops confidence in you. Even routine walks, taken as a matter of course, increase the trust and communication between owner and dog.

How

You acquired Dandy for one principal reason, to bring joy and comfort to you. How can you enjoy a dog any more than when taking him for a walk, playing fetch, catch, Frisbee, or another game? A walk through the woods or on the beach is a quiet time, a time of relaxation. Dandy gives you an excuse to accomplish this; take advantage of it.

You have many options to explore, and if one type of exercise doesn't fill the bill, you should try another. The more things you do with your dog, the more you will learn to communicate with him and enjoy him.

Where

Walking Dandy around the neighborhood will get you acquainted with his little idiosyncrasies. Observe him closely and he will communicate with you. He might look up at you when he scents another dog. If you learn to read his body language, you will come to appreciate his intelligence.

When you walk in the woods, along the beach, or on the desert and he comes upon new animal scents, watch his body attitude, his tail motion, and his ear movements for messages that tell you what he is thinking. Talk to him, keeping a running conversation going during the walk.

A walk provides you both exercise, but more than that, every walk is a training session, a learning experience for master and dog.

Types of Exercise

Running with an Automobile: Many lazy owners try to exercise their dogs without claiming some of the benefit themselves. Taking a drive with your dog is a great idea, but don't expect anything but grief when you decide to let Dandy out of the car and expect him to run alongside it. If he is held by a leash and he trips or stumbles, he could wind up under a wheel. If he is running free, he might run in front of your vehicle or another car, with disastrous results. At best, exercising your dog alongside your car is risky, and at worst, it might cost the life of your dog.

Bicycling: Although biking is pretty good exercise for you, it could be too strenuous for Dandy. Even though *you* are powering the bike, it gives you a significant mechanical advantage over walking, jogging, or running.

Biking with your dog can be hazardous to his health and yours if he

suddenly sees another dog and jerks one way or another, upsetting the bike, spilling you, and becoming tangled in the wreckage. You can't communicate well while keeping your eye on the trail and avoiding holes and other obstacles.

Another thought has to do with training. Dandy receives muscle-building exercise but is unable to use his mind as he runs beside your bike. Exercise is enforced, but communication is absent. If you decide to exercise him on your bike, take him for regular walks as well.

Running or Jogging: These human activities usually provide safe exercise for your dog. Best suited to the very active working and sporting breeds, running or jogging with Dandy will certainly give him ample conditioning. These activities don't allow much communication between dog and master, but if he enjoys it, the time is well spent.

Swimming: Swimming is a type of exercise particularly enjoyed by large breeds, although nearly every dog can benefit. Tossing a tennis ball into a lake and telling Dandy to fetch it is an activity he will surely enjoy. Be sure the body of water you're using is safe from currents or physical hazards such as broken bottles or tin cans, and is not a wildlife haven.

Yard Ball: A yard ball is a firm, hollow plastic ball of a circumference large enough that Dandy can't pick it up. He will probably love to bat it around with his muzzle. Such a toy is readily available from pet supply stores and catalogs. Many dogs will entertain themselves for half an hour before tiring of the play. To be effective, the yard ball should be kept from Dandy between sessions.

Exercising Your Dog Off Lead

When should a dog be exercised off lead? Only you can answer this question. Naturally, Dandy should be trained to instantly and almost automatically come when called. He should be well canine-socialized; he surely will meet other dogs on occasion. We'll hope the dog he meets is not a female in heat, unless he's been neutered. He should carry proper identification because he may become separated from you, regardless of his training. He should be taught to behave around strangers that he's bound to meet around the next corner. He should not be aggressive toward wildlife; the next animal he meets may be a deer, a skunk, or worse, a porcupine.

If you have developed trust in your dog in every way, and have thought of all the possible situations he might encounter in the area in which you are allowing him off lead, go for it if you must. A better idea is to invest in a retractile lead, or simply fasten a long nylon cord to his collar.

Breeding Your Bitch

There are many good books available to assist you in the dog breeding process. Here, we will try to discourage you from this program.

The reasons supporting breeding are:

• Your bitch is of the highest possible quality, which means you have invested in a show- and breeding-quality purebred.

• She is an outstanding example of her breed and has no hereditary faults.

• You have proven or are proving her merits in the show ring.

• You can afford the costs associated with breeding her and raising puppies.

• You have found a proven high-quality stud dog that will compliment her minimal faults.

• You have adequate facilities for breeding and raising a litter.

• You have and are prepared to spend the time required to take care of a brood bitch and her litter.

• You have the necessary contacts to place all the puppies in good homes.

If you can honestly say you have all these factors covered, you certainly don't want to have her spayed.

Five Poor Reasons for Breeding Dogs

1. She will make a better pet (or hunting dog, companion, guard dog, and so on) if she has a litter. This is unfounded in fact and untrue.

2. She will get fat if she isn't bred once. This is a cop-out for poor nutritional planning. Dogs get fat for the same reason people do: If they are in normal health, fat dogs simply have consumed more calories than their bodies need. If you monitor your bitch's activities, and adjust her diet accordingly, she won't get fat whether spayed or not.

3. "I want my children to witness the *miracle of birth*." The odds are, they won't actually see the birth, and if they do, they won't enjoy it. Even if your children manage to witness the birth of a pup or two, what are you going to do with the litter of puppies once they are born? If education is truly your motive, rent or buy a properly narrated video of childbirth. Videos are also available that include the birth of many animals, both domestic and wild. Some of those films are diagrammatically illustrated for teaching purposes.

4. Puppies are cute. True, but puppies are also an obligation, a commitment. The world is saturated with too many dogs that were once cute puppies. Millions of these dogs wind up in shelters and pounds, unwanted, unloved, waiting to die after their brief stay in cramped cages. Others manage to avoid dog wardens and survive like jackals in the alleys of our cities. If they can avoid being maimed or killed by traffic, they live by their wits, scavenge from dumpsters, and serve as a reservoir of disease for our pets.

5. "I want another puppy exactly like my dog." This, of course, is impossible to achieve. Dogs are individuals, and no two are identical. The best you can hope for is a puppy with half its genes from the well-loved dam. Leave dog breeding to the experts who study the genetic makeup of dogs and are able to produce superior puppies from carefully selected gene pools.

Spaying

Although this isn't usually considered a part of routine dog care, it certainly should be. Spaying your female pet may extend her life and prevent diseases. It usually results in a dog that is easier to handle and one that is under less stress.

Age to Spay

Female companion dogs should be spayed before their first heat, at or before six months of age.

Benefits of Spaying

A spay operation is a surgical procedure in which both ovaries and the uterus are removed. It stops her estrous cycle before it begins, she won't come into heat every six months, and it permanently prevents her from becoming pregnant.

Spaying at an early age is the best way to prevent the formation of breast cancer later in life and will prevent the life-threatening disease known as pyometra (see page 111). This operation doesn't change her personality or growth and development rate.

Castration

Castration, sometimes called neutering, entails the surgical removal of both testicles. It is a safe procedure done under general anesthetic by your veterinarian.

When to Neuter

This operation can be done at any age, but should be accomplished by the time Dandy reaches sexual maturity at six or eight months.

Benefits

The aggressive male is usually easier to handle when neutered and has one less thing on his mind when training begins. Castrated males usually wander less, spend less time calculating a way to escape from the yard, and are less often found in packs of roaming dogs. Further discussion on this subject is found in the chapter on health, beginning on page 92.

Purebred neutered males and spayed females are welcome in obedience shows, agility trials, tracking trials, and practically every other dog activity except showing and field trials.

Chapter Five

Canine Nutrition

Water

Fresh drinking water must be supplied for Daisy all her life. Other nutritional elements may be varied under different circumstances, but a source of clean water is always essential. That doesn't mean adding clean water to a dirty pan. Dogs, like humans, prefer cool water, served fresh in a clean pan.

History of Dog Food

Where did dog foods originate? Are they any good? Can I feed table scraps? If people food is good enough for me, why can't my dog eat it?

James Spratt, an American entrepreneur from Cincinnati, abandoned his former employment in lightning rod sales and invented dog food. In 1860 he was traveling in England when he got the idea, and his first food was Spratt's Dog Cake. It was made from blended wheat meals, vegetables, beetroot, and meat.

Walker, Harrison, and Garthwaite, a packaging company that served the English foxhound trade, manufactured his product. Spratt later opened a plant in New York City and the American dog food industry was born.

Government Agencies

After establishment in the United States, as one might expect, regulation and standardization of the dog food industry began.

NRC: Today, the National Research Council of the National Academy of Sciences reviews scientific literature to establish the minimum nutritional needs of dogs. The NRC investigated the nutritional needs of dogs, and realized the need for growing puppies is different from adult maintenance requirements, which, in turn, differ from the dietary needs of dogs under stress. These stressors include training, heavy work such as hunting, pregnancy and lactation, and recuperation and repair from injury.

FDA: The Food and Drug Administration regulates canned foods, additives, and labeling. The FDA also enforces residue and tolerance levels of chemicals, as well as the labels on all dog foods. If a can boasts *beef stew* on the label, it must contain at least 25 percent beef. If it is *beef dinner*, it contains between 25 and 95 percent beef. If the label states the can is beef, it must contain at least 95 percent beef, and an all-beef dog food contains only beef.

The FDA is also responsible for dog food safety. It assures that dog food must be as safe for canines as human foods are for people. This agency also has Good Manufacturing Practice (GMP) rules governing the processing of dog foods.

AAFCO: The Association of American Feed Control Officials is an organization that represents individual state officials. This organization provides testing protocol for manufacturers so they will meet state nutritional quality and safety regulations. The testing is done by means of feeding trials, which are directed by staff veterinarians. The agency requires each label to include a guaranteed analysis, which lists the minimum percent of protein and fat, and the maximum percent of fiber and moisture.

AAFCO provides information to consumers, and regulates such statements on labels as Complete and Balanced. They have two separate nutrient profiles, one for growth and reproduction and one for adult maintenance. The agency also specifies the difference between dry matter basis and *as-fed* basis. To compare dog foods, convert the *as-fed* figures to *dry matter* by deducting the quantity of water or moisture contained in the package.

FTC: The Federal Trade Commission regulates advertising claims, to be sure they are neither false nor misleading.

EPA: The Environmental Protection Agency establishes maximal levels of pesticides or other chemical residues permitted in dog foods.

USDA: Finally, the United States Department of Agriculture gets into the act by regulating the temperature of processing all meat of the 4-D types. This is meat derived from dead, dying, diseased, or disabled animals.

Free-Choice Feeding

Daisy's diet and feeding times need not be chiseled in stone, but regularity in feeding is as important to her health as ample water. For this and other reasons, many dogs benefit from free-choice feeding and free-choice water supply.

In case you aren't familiar with the term, *free-choice* means leaving at least a one-day supply of premium dry dog food where it is accessible to Daisy at all times. If she is a house dog, free-choice feeding may be an option. An outdoor dog can also be fed free-choice if a dry place is available where her food supply can be kept without becoming contaminated or eaten by neighborhood dogs.

If Daisy is started on free-choice feeding when you first take her home, she will probably never overeat; however, some dogs insist upon eating every morsel they can find. If Daisy is such a dog, free-choice feeding isn't practical. Other factors to consider when deciding on free-choice feeding are the number of dogs living in your home, the presence of flies and other insects that affect sanitary considerations, and very young children who might munch on the dog's food.

Feeding Frequency

When your seven-week-old puppy arrives in your home, she should be fed free-choice premium dry puppy food, plus two small daily meals of canned and dry food mixed. Gradually increase the quantity of these moist meals as she grows. This schedule should be continued until Daisy is six months old. From six months to a year, feed her one moist meal per day, together with free-choice dry food. After a year, most dogs will maintain quite nicely on free-choice dry food exclusively.

If free-choice feeding isn't a viable option for your dog(s), feed Daisy premium dry puppy food, moistening it with a little water and a bit of canned premium puppy food. She should be fed three times daily while a puppy, and twice daily when she is six months to a year of age.

When she's a year old, her diet can gradually be changed to a premium adult dry food ration, fed once or twice daily. Canned food may be continued for flavor, or dry food can be fed exclusively.

During training, or any time Daisy is working hard, she needs more nutrition than is provided by her maintenance allowance. A good way to determine her dietary requirements is to weigh her weekly. If she is not gaining weight as a puppy or if she is losing weight as an adult, increase her dietary intake. If she is fully grown and you find she is gaining weight, reduce her daily diet accordingly.

Cost of Dog Food

When calculating the cost of feeding your new dog, the price tag doesn't necessarily tell the whole story. What some owners fail to recognize is that a dog's physical and mental condition, performance, longevity, general health, and energy are directly related to diet. Therefore, if you want Daisy to thrive and get the most from life, don't pinch the dog food budget.

Canine nutrition discussions should begin with a tired old adage: If the cost sounds too good to be true, it probably is. The price per pound of any dog food reflects the quality and cost of its constituents and the research that went into its formulation. You must also add the cost of advertising, including in many cases actors' salaries and TV production costs. Dog food is part of a huge industry; the price reflects stockholder profits, directors' salaries, manufacturer, wholesaler, and retailer markups. Keep these in mind when you shop for dog food.

Beware of buying dry dog food from stores that have low product turnover, and don't buy excessive quantities at one time. If Daisy is a Chihuahua, buy the smallest package available. Dry dog food deteriorates with age and should be kept in airtight containers once a sack is opened. It is less expensive in 50-pound (23-kg) bags, but storage takes its toll on nutrients when they are exposed to the air. Fats may become rancid, fat-soluble vitamins A, D, E, and K deteriorate, and some B complex vitamins may be lost.

A few dry dog foods are preserved with natural anti-oxidants such as vitamins C and E, and contain no artificial preservatives. Such foods will usually cost more and may or may not prove to be better sources of nutrition than those containing chemical preservatives, which help maintain palatability and protect foods from early oxidation.

Bagged dog food should not be stored in warm places; elevated temperatures speed deterioration of its ingredients.

Bioavailability

This term refers to the quantity of a food constituent that is actually used by the dog for energy. If an essential dietary element is fed to a dog in a form that is not biologically available, it might as well be left on the store shelf.

When a food is completely burned in a laboratory device known as a *calorimeter*, it releases a specified amount of energy. However, when eaten by an animal, a significant part of the food isn't digested (burned) and is excreted in feces. The difference between energy consumed and the amount excreted in feces is the *apparent digestible energy*. From this is deducted the energy excreted in urine, and this establishes the *metabolizable energy*. This figure defines the bioavailability of nutrients contained in a dog food.

Small dogs require more energy per pound than giants do. Growing puppies require about twice the energy of adults. Pregnancy stress during the last two weeks of gestation may call for an increase of 50 to 60 percent more energy than normal dietary requirements. Working sled dogs in polar conditions require 50 to 100 percent more energy than the average dog does. Racing Greyhounds require up to 20 percent more energy when they are in training and on the track.

Since the bioavailability of every food can't be calculated for Daisy, we must use some practical measurement of the value of a dog food. Therefore, we recommend selecting a name brand food and feeding her a quantity that produces a thrifty body condition. This means weighing Daisy regularly, running your hands over her ribs, and using a discerning eye. If you can feel her ribs through a thin fat cover, her coat is glossy, her eyes are bright, and she is curious and active, her diet is probably fine. If you have any doubt, consult with your veterinarian.

Essential Dietary Requirements

In these days of low-fat human diets, we see people reading package labels more than ever before. Unfortunately, most of us don't pay nearly as much attention to what we feed our dogs.

Fats

Whether or not you're eating a low-fat diet, you must make sure that adequate fat is included in Daisy's diet.

Kcal is a nutritional/metabolic abbreviation for kilocalorie or large calorie. It is a measure of the amount of energy produced by food when oxidized in the body. By strict definition, a Kcal is the amount of heat energy required to raise 1 kg of water from 15 to 16°C.

Dietary fat is a calorie-dense nutrient containing all the essential fatty acids. It contains 9-Kcal energy per gram, more than twice that of carbohydrates or proteins. This occasionally creates a problem. Dogs will usually eat less of a high-fat diet, which may result in shorting themselves on protein, vitamins, and minerals. This is especially true in young puppies.

Animal fats and vegetable oils contain identical calories per gram. These two sources of fat differ principally in palatability; both provide adequate fatty acids for the dog. Adult maintenance foods should contain a minimum of 5 percent fat, including 1 percent linoleic fatty acid. A higher concentration of fat may be desirable in dog foods to improve coats or to improve palatability.

Protein

Canines are not strict carnivores, but Daisy prefers to be a meat-eater. Amino acids (protein components) from vegetables have lower bioavailability than those derived from animal proteins. Relative to optimum canine nutrition, plant protein is therefore of lower quality than animal protein. Adult maintenance diets should contain about 18 percent protein, including specific amounts of ten essential amino acids.

These essential amino acids, which can't be manufactured by the dog and must be supplied in food are: arginine, histidine, isoleucine, leucine, lysine, methionine, phenylalanine, threonine, tryptophan, and valine. Deficiency of any of these amino acids results in dull hair coat, antibody formation reduction, growth suppression, weight loss, musculature wasting, and eventual death.

Too much protein can be equally as bad as too little. It must be balanced with the energy content of the diet: 15 percent dietary protein is usually considered too little for growing puppies; 20 percent is generally sufficient. Following weaning, the dietary protein requirement is gradually decreased. Increased demands are seen during pregnancy, lactation, and work. In aged dogs, protein requirements are low and, if high quantities are fed, may aggravate compromised kidneys.

Carbohydrates

Carbohydrates (starches) also are sources of calories derived from plant tissues. Unlike humans, dogs have an insignificant nutritional requirement for carbohydrates, but it's impractical to produce dog foods without them. (Starches are an inexpensive source of calories.) Dog foods that are high in *plant* carbohydrates and contain *plant* protein and *plant* fat are not recommended. A food combining animal protein with plant carbohydrates and fats is generally preferred nutrition for a dog.

Minerals

A specified amount of 12 different essential minerals are listed in the AAFCO nutrient requirements in specified percentages. The NRC *Nutrient Requirements of Dogs* reports on the role of two of these important minerals. In order to provide the optimal mineral balance, the diet should contain a ratio of 1.2 parts calcium to 1 part phosphorus (up to 1.4 to 1). The sources of these minerals is also significant.

Vitamins

The AAFCO advises that 11 vitamins in specified quantities should be included in adult maintenance diets. If you are a vitamin buff, you will be interested to learn that vitamin C is not one of these. Dogs have the ability to manufacture vitamin C in sufficient quantities, and therefore require no external source of this vitamin.

Vitamin A is toxic in extremely high doses, and its use should be considered with care, although it is often prescribed in safe doses for various diseases.

Vitamin D requirements are dependent on the dietary concentration of calcium and phosphorus. Likewise, the requirement for vitamin E is related to the intake of fatty acids.

Rather than discuss each vitamin independently, it is probably best to state that the requirements and results of excessive or insufficient intake are covered in the NRC book mentioned above. For those who wish to try to formulate their own kitchen diets, please read the NRC book.

Supplements

A complete and balanced diet, such as a *premium* dry dog food, needs no vitamin or mineral supplementation. By the same token, it's a mistake to feed a bargain brand dog food and hope to cover its inadequacies with inexpensive vitamin-mineral supplements.

Dietary supplements are sometimes used to improve a dog's coat and make it more glossy. Such coat conditioners, usually containing fatty acids, are rarely necessary and have marginal benefit. They are usually harmless, however, and may be prescribed by veterinarians to compensate for stresses. The best way to attain and maintain a shiny coat with rich colors is through sound nutrition, not a bottle of coat enhancer. Check with your veterinarian before you use lecithin, vitamin A, corn oil, or other coat-enhancing preparations.

Meats

In the past, quality and bioavailability of protein in dog foods were sometimes suspect. Nutritionists of yesteryear recommended adding bone meal and meat, especially liver or tripe, to dogs' diets. Remembering those recommendations, dog owners often make the mistake of mixing meat with their dog's otherwise excellent foods. Complete and balanced diets have been formulated to provide total nutrition for our dogs, and it is no longer necessary or advisable to supplement.

Prepared Dog Foods

Today's food is a far cry from Spratt's by-guess-and-by-golly formulation, but packaged dog food is the most practical way to feed Daisy.

In order to know which specific food to buy, you must learn how to read a dog food label. Cute televi-sion ads typically show a litter of beautiful puppies or well-trained dogs lying about displaying their glossy coats. Other dog stars are trained to jump over one another or talk by special effects animation. They get your attention, but when you buy their product, keep in mind that you're paying those actors' salaries. All advertising uses marketing tools that affect the product price, but unfortunately, the best advertising doesn't necessarily promote the best dog food.

Labels

Labels are legal documents. Study dog food labels and call or write manufacturers with any questions you may have. Buying a dog food because it's cheaper than others makes about as much sense as buying a product because the dog in the ad was well trained. The *sources* and *quality* of protein, carbohydrate, and fat are as important as the quantities.

Every product label must list its composition. If it doesn't, pick another dog food. Ingredients are listed according to quantity; that is, if meat and meat by-products are listed first, those products are in greater quantity than ingredients that follow. If soy flour is listed first, soy flour is the leading ingredient in the food.

If a label states that a dog food meets the recommendations of the NRC, it may apply only to canine *maintenance* requirements. Such a food should be adequate for maintaining dogs under minimal stress, and may not be acceptable for growing puppies, performance dogs, or breeding animals. It doesn't supply the increased energy demands of work, training, growth, pregnancy, or lactation.

Labels often specify the *total quantities* of nutrients, not the *bioavailable* nutrients. In such a case, a letter or phone call to the manufacturer is indicated if you are interested in the product. If you receive an inadequate response, choose another product.

The ingredient list should list the source of protein contained in the food. Protein of vegetable origin such as wheat, corn, or soy flour may provide an excellent total protein analysis on the package, but it may be misleading if that protein is not bioavailable.

Feeding Trials

Some foods, usually the premium brands, will include a label declaration stating the food has passed the AAFCO feeding trials for the entire life cycle of canines. These products should contain the right amount of bioavailable food elements required for puppies, youths, and working adults.

If the AAFCO declaration isn't shown, it doesn't necessarily mean the food hasn't been subjected to feeding trials. Call or write to the manufacturer and ask for reports of feeding trial results, and ask about the sources of protein and fat. Ask if the formula is kept constant, regard-less of the seasonal variation of ingredient costs.

If you are unable to understand the information provided by the manufacturers, consult with your veterinarian. If he or she isn't able to help you make an informed decision, borrow a text on the subject. Most veterinary clinics have reference sources for the nutritional requirements of dogs.

Types

There are three general types of dog foods available, canned, semi-moist, and dry. Each has its advantages and drawbacks.

Canned: Of the three types of dog foods presently on the market, canned foods are usually the most expensive per pound, but they store well and are highly palatable. Feeding canned food alone may not give Daisy an adequate amount of roughage in her diet and may predispose her to urinary frequency. Canned food contains more than 60 percent water, and some have preservatives that may cause a diuretic effect when fed exclusively. The meat contained in canned dog foods often isn't the highest quality, in spite of what dog food commercials would have you believe. In fact, some canned foods contain virtually no meat. It is amazing what scientists can do to the appearance of soybeans.

Semimoist: Consumer appeal is the principal selling point of soft-moist or semimoist foods. In their plastic packages they look like ground meat, but they rarely contain any appreciable quantity of animal protein. Semimoist foods don't store as well as canned or dry foods, are expensive, and often contain rather large amounts of sugars and some questionable chemical preservatives.

Feeding semimoist foods often leads to greater water consumption, which results in frequent urination. Semimoist foods are also often incriminated as the cause for certain allergic reactions.

Dry: Dry foods have several advantages over the other two types. They are usually the least expensive diet for Daisy and are often the best nutrition for your dollar. Daisy can live a healthy and active life on an exclusive diet of premium dry dog food and water. All dry foods are not alike, however; they vary greatly in terms of ingredient quality, nutritional content, and palatability. If you carefully choose a dry food for her regular diet, it shouldn't be necessary to flavor Daisy's food or to add supplements to make it a complete and balanced diet.

Premium Brands

Excellent premium dog foods are available in pet supply stores, supermarkets, and from veterinarians. Nutritional information on these packages will specify whether the product provides optimum nutrients for growth in puppies, for reproduction, for working dogs, adult maintenance, or all stages of canine life.

Premium brands are usually the most expensive dry dog foods on the market, yet they are often the most economical to feed. Their high nutritional content per pound often means you feed less quantity, and the dog produces less voluminous stools. These foods are usually quite palatable and well accepted by dogs. In most cases, premium foods may be offered free-choice.

To increase palatability, a basic diet of a premium complete and balanced dry food may be mixed with premium canned food of the same quality.

Commercial Brands

Commercial foods are those found stacked on the shelves of grocery stores, feed stores, supermarkets, and discount stores. Many of them provide excellent nutrition, and some of the name brands have been on the market for decades. Any discussion of these commercial foods is relative, since they number in the hundreds and vary greatly in quality. As a general rule, you might wish to contact the manufacturer and ask for the data on the food being considered. You should receive a report of the bioavailability of the constituents, any feeding trials being conducted, the sources of all the ingredients, and the analysis.

Generic Brands

Generic brands should always be considered, but before buying, be sure the food conforms to the standards discussed in the preceding paragraphs. Generic foods may vary in composition from month to month, as various grains or other ingredients become more or less available. Rarely will generic foods be proven in feeding trials due to the expense of those trials.

If you decide to use a generic food, ask the food manager which food has the most rapid turnover, read the label, check the ingredients, and make your selection.

Homemade Diets

The family kitchen is a poor place to formulate your dog's food, and the use of homemade diets often leads to nutritional problems. You are advised to leave dog food production to those who have analytical laboratories, research facilities, and feeding trials to prove their products.

Formulated Rations

Puppy Rations

These dog foods are formulated especially for growing puppies and should furnish adequate nutrition for normal muscle development and bone growth of the young dog. Like other rations, you will probably get only what you pay for. Just because the food is labeled for puppies, doesn't mean you shouldn't do your homework. The same rules apply regarding quality, and the sources of constituents are as important as the percentages. Feeding trials are also done on puppy food, and the

AAFCO label should be found on puppy rations.

Breeding and Whelping Rations

Brood bitches require additional food when they are under the stress of heat, pregnancy, whelping, and nursing. The diet is increased at certain times and decreased at other times of the breeding cycle. Don't change diets; consult your veterinarian or a book on dog breeding such as Barron's *Complete Book of Dog Breeding*, by Dan Rice.

Working and Training Rations

The same precautions apply to dogs in intensive training or work. Diet change is not necessary, but the quantity and number of feedings per day is increased to compensate for the additional calories being used.

Special Health Rations

Special diets are available for dogs with kidney disease, diabetes, gastritis, flatulence, and other health problems. Consult your veterinarian before you use these foods.

Treats

All dogs receive a certain amount of extra food in the form of treats. Commercial dog treats usually don't upset the dog, and if Daisy isn't gaining weight and has a normal appetite, treats are fine in minimal quantity.

Chewing sticks is dangerous, but these mischievous Jacks don't seem to care.

For treats, you can use low-calorie biscuits or other tasty dry products. Tiny pieces of baked liver or small bits of well-done roast beef are favorite treats among handlers, but in sufficient quantity; they can throw a dog's nutritional balance out of whack. You be the judge. If Daisy's weight is constant, she shows no dietary upsets, and she responds well to your particular choice, stay with it. Remember to keep meat treats in a plastic bag to prevent contamination while in your pocket, and refrigerate them when not training.

Dietary No-Nos

Milk will usually bring on a bout of diarrhea, as will organ meat (liver, heart, kidney), rich foods, and table scraps. Avoid feeding these items. Cooked bones are another attractive dietary nuisance. Chicken or chop bones, steak bones, ribs, and some roast bones may splinter when Daisy chomps down on them. Bone shards can lodge in the dog's mouth or throat or they can be swallowed where they can cause other medical problems. Ice cream, candy, pizza, potato chips, peanuts, and a host of other human junk foods are difficult for the dog to digest and should also be avoided.

Important Warning: Stay away from *chocolate*; it can poison your dog.

Obesity and Inappropriate Eating Habits

If Daisy is a glutton and tends to be fat, you must take the responsibility of feeding her meals that will maintain her condition. If she is housed with another dog, it will be necessary to separate them at mealtime. Measured amounts should be fed and the dog's weight and condition should be monitored frequently.

Obesity may also be handled in a young dog by adding low-calorie fillers to her diet. Ground carrots, canned green beans, or other low-calorie foods may be added to her balanced diet without upsetting it appreciably.

Older obese dogs may just be lazy, and when a dog begins to age and no longer exercises every day, her food must be cut back. It's important to reevaluate her nutritional needs when you begin the cutback program, since nutritional requirements change with age. High-quality food, fed in reduced quantity will usually control an old dog's obesity.

A sudden weight gain accompanied by a voracious appetite is cause for alarm. There are a number of health problems, including diabetes, that may be to blame.

If Daisy looks skinny, but has a good appetite and boundless energy, don't despair. Some dogs are so ambitious and energetic that they remain thin all their lives. They burn all the calories their diets furnish, and store none. It's best to feed such dogs premium foods—free-choice—or frequent small meals of dry food mixed with canned food each day. If you see a continued weight loss or loss of energy in a thin dog, if her coat becomes dry, or she shows any other signs of ill health, consult your veterinarian.

Readers who wish to learn more about canine nutrition can purchase *Nutritional Requirements of Dogs*, Revised, from the National Research Council, telephone 1-800-624-6242. This inexpensive volume is updated regularly and will answer virtually all of your technical questions about canine nutrition.

Chapter Six

Training

This section frequently refers to puppies, but the same ideas apply to grown dogs as well. If your new dog is several months or years old, he may need none or some of this training, depending on his past experiences.

Training begins the day Dandy arrives in your home. As we have discussed, being held and cuddled is part of bonding and a form of learning. The single most important training tenant is to *encourage Dandy to focus his attention on you*. Get and hold his concentration on your face, hands, and voice. Call him by name every time you meet him. Soon you will see that he is concentrating and listening for your voice.

Behavior

What is canine behavior? It is the way Dandy conducts himself in, or responds to, his environment. It may be acceptable, or it may be atrocious. Behavior is what a dog does when he is alone or in human or other canine company. If measured in human society, behavior is the dog's comportment when he is in human homes and human environments.

Behavior Modification

This sophisticated-sounding term is used to describe changing a dog's behavior from bad to better through application of the principals of conditioning, using rewards and reinforcements. In some cases, it's conditioning to the extent that his reaction to your voice becomes a reflex. Appropriate training is the first step toward behavioral modification.

Pack Instincts and Dominance

Dogs are pack-oriented; they look to the pack leader, or alpha dog, for guidance and direction. In order to teach Dandy, you must establish yourself as the *leader* of his pack. You aren't his equal; you are his mentor, his supervisor, his boss, and you must assume the role of alpha dog in his new pack.

Proof of your dominance should be firmly established, even in little things, such as when you pick him up. He may wish to be put down immediately, but you should hold him for a few minutes, scratching and petting him. He will not only associate the pleasure of your petting with being held or being called to you, he will realize his submission doesn't hurt. It is critical for Dandy to learn very early that you are the pack leader.

When Dandy comes to you, whether you have called him or not, you should reward him with a soft "good dog," a pat on the head, and a scratch behind the ears. This establishes the fact that you like him to come to you, and when he does so, he's rewarded with praise and petting.

When Dandy does something you like, give him your approval. When he does something wrong, don't make a big issue of it. To do so will give him a means to get your attention, and he might repeat the mis-

Trust must be established before agility games are attempted.

take whenever he feels neglected. *Dogs would rather be scolded than ignored.* Your plan must be to praise good behavior and ignore bad behavior.

A puppy has cognitive ability at a very early age, and learning continues throughout life. There is reason to believe that the more training a dog experiences, the greater will be his capacity to learn. Or, to put it another way, it's possible that when a dog is kept on the leading edge of the learning curve, he will never lose his capacity to learn new things.

Try never to give Dandy a foolish command or assign him a task he can't perform. Remember the canine pack mentality. He trusts you to start him in the right direction, and to keep him on the right track. He learns you will always reward him with your love and approval for a job well done.

Dominance Training: You can demonstrate your dominance, whether your new dog is a pup or an adult, by certain actions. Dominance training doesn't mean abuse—you need never scold, strike, or apply undue force:

• Make Dandy move out of your way when you walk from room to room.

• Pick him up and remove him from a chair, or his favorite spot in the room, and take his place.

• If he eats in the house, feed him after you have eaten, and don't tolerate begging at your table.

• Ignore him occasionally when you first come home and reserve your greeting for a few minutes later.

- Keep his favorite toys out of his reach and give him one as a special treat; play with him, then put the toy away.
- Don't allow him on your bed or in the bedroom except when he's specifically invited.
- Occasionally tie him in the yard while you are busily working around him.

Pack dominance may be carried even further. When beginning a relationship with a *grown* dog, or with an aggressive or domineering puppy, handle him frequently and extensively:
- Sit on the ground and hold him on your lap.
- Touch every part of his body, including his paws, tail, belly, and back.
- Rub his ears, talk in a soothing manner, and repeat his name time and again.
- Open his mouth, and hold it open for a few seconds.
- Turn Dandy on his back while you rub his tummy and stretch his legs, first one then another. He will soon accept you as the pack leader, and will take a subservient role in the family.

This technique may be more difficult when handling an older dog that is new to your family, and you should certainly slow down the process and take your time accomplishing it. Whatever the age of the dog, use the same approach. Regardless of how long it takes, it will work, and will be an excellent way to gain Dandy's trust, and at the same time to establish dominance.

Dominance training is important, even in small dogs.

As he matures, make a point of taking away Dandy's food bowl while he is eating, then take him for a walk around the yard before you allow him to continue eating. Teach him to come and to sit very early in life. This will further establish your dominance over him and solidify your role as pack leader.

Trainability and Intelligence

Trainability is a measure of a dog's ability and desire to learn, his wish to please his master, and the ease with which he takes direction. It is associated with personality, which is partially genetic and partly learned.

Dominance Training Techniques

- Take food away for a few minutes at your discretion.
- After playing, take toys away and put them out of sight.
- Win tug-of-war games at least 60 percent of the time.
- Always dictate what game you will play and when.
- Occasionally tie the dog in the yard for an hour.
- Move the dog from his resting place and take his place.
- Open the dog's mouth for a short time; examine his teeth.
- Hold his jaws closed with your hand.
- Lay the dog on his back and scratch his belly.
- Touch each part of the dog's body.
- Flex and extend all his leg joints.
- Part his toes and massage the pads and webs.
- Feed him after the humans have eaten.
- Never allow him on the beds.
- Don't allow him on the furniture.
- Teach *come*, *sit*, and *down* early in life.

Intelligence is a measure of the dog's problem-solving ability. In the best of all worlds, exceptional intelligence will be coupled with a highly trainable personality.

When training, don't confuse the dog. Give him short, concise, explicit commands on which he can concentrate, and thus understand. Never give a command for a task he is physically or mentally incapable of performing. Early in any training, make his tasks simple, gradually increasing the difficulty as he grasps the simple endeavors.

Body Language

Patience and careful observation on your part will lead you to appreciate Dandy's signals, and soon you'll notice him reading and understanding yours. You will be able to tell when he is processing your command in his mind and deciding how to do the task you've given him. His response to your command is twofold: He will first signal you he understands, then he will obey. His body language, facial expression, tail carriage, and limb movement all have meanings.

Work-Play Balance

You can't teach the dog; you can only lead him to learn what actions you expect from him. Take care not to bore or tire Dandy in any training exercise; endless repetitions of a particular activity are counterproductive. All puppies have quite short attention spans, so keep the lessons even shorter. Repeating your first lesson two or three times is sufficient for one session. Never repeat any task *until he learns it*. Such an attitude will only tire and bore him.

Commands and Rewards

A reward is anything Dandy likes, whether it is a pat on the head, a scratch behind the ear, a kind word, or a special tidbit from your hand.

Almost right is still wrong. Never reward Dandy simply for trying, or he will never get it right. When an exercise is not done correctly, simply change the subject. Don't scold or make a big issue of his failure. Instead, when he fails, pick up his leash and take him for a walk. Forget the lesson for a day and spend a few minutes with him doing an exercise he has already learned.

Probably, his failure is due to lack of understanding of what you want accomplished. When dealing with failures, accept at least half the blame yourself. Try to figure out a better way to teach the task.

Once Dandy completely understands what his job is, his desire to please will lead him to success. Affection between owner and dog can't be faked; if you love your dog, you will show it. If you treat Dandy fairly, and demonstrate your love at all times, he will bond with you like glue. He may show similar affection for your spouse and your children,

but his ties are strongest to his mentor, the person with whom he spends the most productive time.

If you've obtained an older dog, spend a week teaching him to respond to his new name. Discover what tasks he has already learned. See if he responds to the *fetch, catch,* or *hide-and-seek* command. Give him some elementary obedience commands and watch his response to *heel, sit, stay,* or *come.* When you attempt to teach him a task he resents or will not immediately perform, take him for a walk on his leash. Then start all over with a task you know he can do well. When he performs this exercise correctly, lavish praise on him.

While in a training mode, you should never give Dandy a command you can't enforce or a task he is unable to perform. Take care not to put him into situations where his actions can be arbitrary and he can easily disobey. For instance, when he is still a puppy, and you tell him to sit from across the room, Dandy may decide to remain standing. This constitutes negotiation on his part, and puts you in an untenable situation. Don't resort to yelling "SIT" at the top of your voice; if you do, you can expect negative results.

Methods of Training

You may have heard that there is only one correct way to train a dog.

This is absurd! Dogs are individuals. They don't reason alike, and some are quicker to grasp ideas than others. Certain breeds have more capability than others in particular disciplines, but all dogs are trainable. Your job is to find the key to training your new dog.

The Value of Rewards

People often approach dog training with their fists full of tidbits. When a particular exercise is performed satisfactorily, the dog is given a bit of cooked liver or some other doggy treat. If this is your plan, fill your pockets with tidbits, and award a yummy every time he obeys and performs according to direction. This type of reward system may or may not enhance training, but is usually more applicable to exercises such as *sit, down, heel,* and so on.

Another training method is to bond so well with your dog that he will respond to you and expect no other reward than your praise and petting for his successes. This bonding response should always be your goal.

Obedience training, or any of the other disciplines outlined in this book, can be taught without treats. If Dandy is strongly bonded to you, he will be happy to perform for your affection, which you must never fail to give. Dandy will work hard for a certain gentle voice modulation, which he will come to recognize as your ultimate approval. Your "good dog," or "good boy," will mean more to him than any tidbit.

Dandy is likely to enjoy learning new things, and new experiences are often sufficient reward to maintain his enthusiasm. However, it never hurts to add a couple of "attaboy's."

If you wish to offer some tasty performance reward, it should be very small and should be offered at odd times, not every time he does a task well. You must never let him know when to expect the tidbit reward. If you have begun training with food rewards, try to phase them out as you move into more complicated tasks.

The most important thing to remember about training is to get and hold Dandy's attention. Without his unceasing *focus* on you and your commands, you're spinning your wheels.

Focus is the key to agility training.

Basics

If Dandy happily runs to you and affectionately jumps up and stains your clothes, what is your reaction going to be? Think about it: He came to you; how can you reprimand him for such action? Surely he must be punished for jumping up; you can't tolerate the action, can you? Just look at the mud on your slacks. What do you do in this and similar situations? Read on.

Communication

Dogs, even when still puppies, have the capacity to think, reason, and plan. They haven't the ability to understand complex statements, and their capacity for abstract thinking is probably poor; thus, we must use some fundamental tools.

Associative Learning

Associative learning is a type of learning that relates an action to a reaction. The simplest example of associative learning is when Dandy behaves and you pet him. He does something and you react to it immediately. He connects his action (behaving) to your reaction (petting).

Dandy associates the reward he receives with a particular desirable action he performed on command. The reward may be an edible treat, a kind word, a pat on the head, or scratching behind his ears.

Associative learning may also be negative, such as when Dandy performs inappropriately and meets with your obvious disapproval signified by your ignoring him. Dandy must learn that his inappropriate behavior, at the very best, leads nowhere and gets him nothing.

Punishment or Negative Reinforcement

Punishment usually refers to negative reinforcement of a command or your negative reaction to his action. It is used by some inexperienced trainers as a means of dissuading a dog from repeating an incorrect response to training, and its use is a judgment error in most instances.

A gentle tightening of the training collar without a spoken word has a much more lasting effect on Dandy than yelling, nagging, or jerking the collar.

Verbal correction can be a form of punishment or even abuse when it is frequently repeated, especially when it is joined with a physical action.

Inappropriate discipline or punishment may cause Dandy to do anything to escape training. It can cause him to shun you and avoid your training sessions by running away.

Hitting the dog or yelling at him when he doesn't obey a command is an example of negative association. Another example of negative reinforcement is when you yell "NO" at the top of your voice, then throw something at Dandy when you catch him digging in the garden. Such techniques are not only inadvisable, they are usually inhumane and will interfere with your ability to teach him anything.

Remote Negative Reinforcement

Sometimes, mild *remote* negative devices such as squirt guns can be used under certain circumstances. For example: Dandy insists on getting on the furniture when you are out of the room. You don't want him there, but he never jumps on the sofa when you're in the room, and if you aren't there, it's impossible to stop him. If you can direct a stream of water on him through the crack of a door, he may not associate the water with you, but with jumping on the furniture. He will probably remember that experience and refrain from repeating the action.

Playtime

Before discussing any specific training, a word about play. *Playing with Dandy is as important as any lessons you can teach.* Never fail to take time out from training, or to skip training altogether some days, just to play. As you will see later, play can be constructive teaching, but Dandy won't know it. Play might be defined as any activity he truly enjoys.

The younger the pup, the shorter the attention span. Don't expect Dandy to see into the future. He wants to play all the time, but he will take time out for a lesson now and then if you don't insist on taking up too much of his playtime. If every training session is followed by a play period, both owner and dog will be happier!

Manners

Manners might be defined as rules of social conduct according to human customs. Manners include housebreaking, displaying desirable habits, and lack of inappropriate behavior. Manners are the acceptable characteristics or the deportment a dog exhibits in a human environment. Good manners make a dog welcome in your home or the homes of your friends.

In teaching manners, your commands must be simple, and Dandy's response will be simple. Be sure he fully understands what is expected in every case. Don't reprimand or nag him for mistakes he makes. Above all, keep your temper and have patience.

Recall or Come

The first command for Dandy to learn and respond to is his name, and the second is *recall* or the *come* command. He will learn his name by your constant repetition, and come will easily be taught as well.

Take advantage of his natural responses. As you step outside where Dandy is, get his attention by calling his name. As soon as he looks at you, repeat his name and if he begins to run toward you, tell him "come," or if he doesn't, pick up his food bowl, and the instant he begins to come toward you, say "come." When the pup arrives, praise him with exuberant excitement. Build up his confidence. Make him believe he is always right.

You will probably teach Dandy to come at feeding time, and he won't realize he has learned anything. This task is easily taught to a very young pup, and the sooner it is mastered, the better. It should be practiced frequently, until Dandy's recall response is automatic.

If you're dealing with an older dog or if your new dog is a bit stubborn,

fasten a long, lightweight, nylon line to his collar. Allow him to wander away from you some distance. Then, with zeal, drop to one knee and give the command, "Dandy (hesitation), come." If he doesn't respond with the enthusiasm you expect, give a gentle pull on the line, repeating the command. When Dandy arrives on your lap, generously praise him and tell him what a good dog he is. Then release him from the exercise with an "OK."

Repeat the recall command frequently at odd times to catch him off guard. When his response to the command has become automatic, try him off leash, in the fenced yard. Repeat the command several times daily for grooming, feeding, and especially for petting, but *never call Dandy to you to scold or discipline him*. That will defeat your purpose. Instead, each time he comes on command, praise and pet him, regardless what mischief you have called him away from. *Be consistent.* When he comes to you, whether or not you have called, acknowledge his response and reward him. For additional commands, see Fundamentals of Obedience Training, page 80.

Housebreaking

In the first few weeks of life, Dandy did whatever he felt like doing. Urinating, defecating, eating, and playing were all done whenever he had the urge. The nest was his world and those were the behavioral rules by which he lived. Then, one day you selected and carried him

from this utopia to the strange environment of your home and now he must change his manners. How can he do it? How can you expect such a sudden change in his attitude?

He must be caused to think, and think in relation to cause and effect. That's your job, to bring about the thinking process in your puppy. To housebreak Dandy, you must impose human restrictions on his life. You must cause him to "think" like a human. He has no way of knowing about human customs until he is taught; therefore, you should never punish, scold, or otherwise reprimand him for messing on the floor.

Young puppies use little discretion, and when they feel the urge to urinate or defecate, they hardly hesitate a second. The job is finished before you notice, then it's too late to correct. To be effective, your response to a puppy's *accident* must occur within five seconds from the time it happens. After this time, Dandy won't associate his action with any corrective measure you may take.

If you swat Dandy when he is performing a natural act, you will confuse him. Rubbing his nose in his urine isn't likely to make a lasting impression either. Once the act of urination or defecation is begun, it's already gone from Dandy's mind.

Begin housebreaking the day Dandy makes his appearance in your home. When you see him preparing to urinate or defecate on the floor, don't scold, don't yell, or make a big fuss as he prepares to eliminate on the carpet. Instead, pick him up immediately and take him to a designated area of the backyard. Place him on the ground and slowly back off. At first, he will be confused, but if you put him in the same toilet area each time, he will soon realize it is the place for eliminations.

After he has emptied his bladder or bowels in the toilet area, praise him, play with him, and allow him back inside.

When the odors of previous eliminations are established in the toilet area, he will seek out the spot regardless of where he is or what he is doing. Take him to the toilet area immediately after each meal, when he cries at night, as soon as he wakes in the morning, after naps, and before bedtime.

Nighttime Training

Take away Dandy's food and drinking water two hours before lights out. Sometimes a walk late in the evening will cause him to sleep better, and don't forget to take him to his toilet area immediately before he turns in for the night.

Buy a crate (kennel) or well-made wire pen. Place Dandy in his pen or crate containing an old sweater or some other article with your scent, his nylon chew bone, and nothing else. He will object to this confinement, but if you give him a little favor, perhaps a rawhide chewy, he will soon accept the restriction. If he cries, don't scold, tell him "wait," and walk away.

During the night, tend to his whining immediately when he cries. Take him from the pen or crate and carry him to the toilet area of the yard. Don't play with him, pet him, or make a fuss over him in any way. This is a duty trip only. If he defecates or urinates, praise him. Return him to the crate after a few minutes

in the toilet area, whether he has eliminated or not.

Paper Training

Put Dandy in a portable pen in a bathroom or other easily cleaned room. Cover half the floor of the pen with several layers of newspaper, and place his nylon bone, water dish, and bed on the other half. He then has no choice but to use the newspapers for his eliminations. After a week or two, you can remove the pen, but keep him confined in the small room with the newspapers on the floor when you are not with him. In all probability, he will continue to use them, and within a reasonable time he can be trusted to roam about the house, and will return to the papers for eliminations.

Put his papers nearer and nearer to the back door as time goes on. Then pull the papers under the door, with just a corner showing inside the room. He will probably whine to get to the papers, and you should respond by putting him out. Eventually, you will have him housebroken.

Crate Training

If Dandy is an indoor dog, buy a fiberglass crate. Think of it as his den, his place of refuge. One of the first commands to teach Dandy when he arrives in your home is *kennel,* which means he is to go into his crate and stay there.

Never use crating as a punishment for some mischief he's gotten into. Make the association with his crate positive. Praise him when he enters his crate and give him a chew stick, nylon bone, or other treat. Put an article of your unwashed clothing in the crate; he will recognize your scent and it will make him more comfortable. Most dogs enjoy the cavelike atmosphere of a crate when they are sleeping, and a crate often makes a dog a welcome guest in motel rooms when you are traveling.

While Dandy is still a puppy, crate him several times daily for short periods. Once he has been put in the crate, tell him "wait," then walk away, and don't look back. Don't spend an instant telling him "Good-bye"; just close the gate and beat a rapid retreat, ignoring his pleas to follow you. Once he has settled down and accepted his confinement for a while, let him out, praise him, and play with him for a few minutes.

The kennel or crate is used for nighttime confinement while house-breaking Dandy, and it can also be used to shut him away from attractive kitchen odors if he begins begging. He will voluntarily use this den

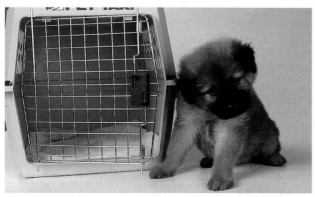

Make sure the crate is large enough for an adult dog.

for napping or to escape the activity of the household when it becomes hectic or irritating.

Games Dogs Play

Some games can teach Dandy tasks without his realizing what you are up to.

Hide-and-Seek

This is a favorite game for any pup and his master, mistress, or children. Two or more people are needed to play this rainy-day or evening sport.

One person holds Dandy very securely while the other goes into another room and hides under a bed, behind a chair, drape, or other object. The holder then releases the pup, telling Dandy "find Kim." If he doesn't understand, have the hiding child softly call Dandy's name once. That should bring immediate results. When Kim is discovered, she can expect to have her face licked, and she should respond with petting and love.

After Dandy has learned the rules of this game, make it more difficult. Have the hiding child go into a closet, but leave the door open an inch. If otherwise safe, expand the hiding places to the backyard, garden shed, or garage.

A variation of the hide-and-seek game uses a toy, one that is reserved for this game. When you begin, name the object, show it to him, and let him smell it. The object is then hidden in another room and he is sent to find it. The command sounds like this: "Dandy, ball. Ball, Dandy." Then, when hidden: "Dandy, find the ball."

Initially, the ball shouldn't be too well hidden so it can be quickly found. Later, when Dandy has mastered the easily found toy, it can be hidden in places that are more difficult to ferret out. Don't make the mistake of hiding it in a cupboard or other place that Dandy has been taught to avoid.

Catch

While Dandy is still a youngster, one exercise he is almost sure to enjoy is a game of catch. You toss a tennis ball, and he either catches it or picks it up. He may work his own variations into this game, such as deciding to play chase, and you can try to catch him and retrieve the ball. Dandy enjoys being chased, and you probably need the exercise too.

After a game is finished, put the ball away. Never leave tennis balls, soft rubber, or foam balls lying around where they can be found and chewed.

Fetch

Fetch is a simple game, an easily understood exercise, usually connected with the instinctive canine propensity to chase anything that moves. Fetching is natural for some dogs, but training depends upon your dog's mental maturity and desire to chase.

Use a different toy from the one used to play catch. A good fetching

Take care when introducing small children to older dogs.

toy is a fabric-covered lightweight object, such as an old sock tied in a knot. This toy should be kept out of his reach except when you're playing the game.

Dandy begins this sport by sitting next to you. Show him the sock, throw it a dozen feet in front of you, and tell him "Dandy, fetch."

His first response will probably be to chase the sock, pick it up, then wonder what he should do with it. Tell him "Dandy, come," and kneel down to his size. That should elicit a quick run to you, but he may drop the sock along the way.

Take him back to it, tell him "pick it up," and walk back with him to your original position. If he lacks enthusiasm in picking it up, try rubbing a hot dog on the sock. If he doesn't pick it up when told, hand it to him or place it in his mouth, being sure he fully understands what you expect him to do.

Fetching comes natural for most hunting dogs.

As an alternative, when he picks up the sock, begin to run away from him, clapping your hands and telling Dandy "come." As he catches up to you, reach down and take the sock from his mouth with the *give* command.

Whenever he brings the sock to you, tell him "give," or "drop," and take the sock from his mouth. If he is reluctant to give it to you or to drop it, offer a little tidbit. He can hardly accept the treat without dropping the sock.

Don't forcibly pull the dummy from his mouth; this is no time to play tug-of-war. Praise him for a job well done, and repeat the exercise.

Collar and Leash

Training Dandy to wear a collar and walk on a leash is imperative, and the earlier you start, the better. There are many methods of training a dog to walk on a leash, but a positive approach should always be taken. Dandy wants to follow you anyway, so all you must do is add a collar, then a leash, and let him follow.

You can purchase a flat buckle collar made of nylon web or leather at a pet supply store. Training collars made of chain or nylon should be used for obedience training, but for elementary leash work in young puppies, a flat collar is fine (see the section on obedience training for more information about collars).

For the first two or three days, leave Dandy's collar on only while you are with him, playing, romping, and doing things new dogs do. After a few days of wearing his collar, he will accept and ignore it. At that point, it's safe to leave the collar on continuously.

When he is accustomed to wearing the collar, snap a short leash on it and let Dandy drag it around while he follows you. Once he is accustomed to dragging the leash, pick it up and take a short walk around the yard, holding the leash loosely. If he wants to chew it, tell him "no" in a conversational tone, and continue. In the beginning, walk backward, coaxing Dandy to follow by extending your fingers to him.

Don't tug at the leash, and never jerk or snap it. Although it's important to let Dandy know who has control of the leash, it should be done in a gentle, encouraging way, never roughly. Take it easy; you are introducing something foreign to his experience and knowledge. Give him praise for following you and he will soon be delighted to frolic along at your side, disregarding the leash.

Pet supply stores have light-weight retractile leads of various lengths. These convenient retracting leashes give Dandy more freedom than standard leashes and may be used after he is accustomed to walking on a lead.

For a week or two, work Dandy on lead in your backyard. Once he has fully accepted the leash, you can exercise him out of his yard, but before you do, *check with your veterinarian to be sure Dandy has received all necessary vaccinations.*

All pups are active, inquisitive, mischievous and energetic—sometimes they misbehave. They aren't automatons; they are intelligent beings, anxious to learn and to please you. Don't make a federal case out of each mistake Dandy makes. He likes to play and have fun, and as a teacher, you should always try to make his education as painless as possible. No single training session should take more than a few minutes. If continued overly long, Dandy will become bored and lose interest. Don't forget to play with him between exercises.

Some Simple Tricks

These tricks are best taught to puppies using food rewards. After Dandy is more mature, he may per-

form for your applause, but it doesn't hurt to treat him to a bite of food when he does well.

Roll Over

You can easily teach this trick to your pup while he's small in stature. It's a cute stunt, one that is willingly learned if he trusts you.

1. Place Dandy chest down on the carpet in front of you.

2. Place one hand between his elbows, palm upward, so you can grasp his legs between your fingers without alarming him.

3. Hold a favorite tidbit in your other hand and let him see and smell the reward. Then extend a forefinger of the hand holding the tidbit and circumscribe a circle in the air in front of his nose. As you do so, tell him "over."

4. With your hand that is resting palm up beneath him, grip his forelegs and chest and rotate his body in the same direction that you have circumscribed in the air.

5. When he has turned over and is once again chest down in front of you, give him the tidbit and plenty of praise.

Take great care not to alarm Dandy! If he is uncomfortable when you grasp him by the forelegs, relax, pet him, and begin again. Don't give him the reward until he has rotated on the floor. In other words, don't reward him for trying, only when he has successfully performed the trick.

If he seems frightened when you roll him over, or becomes alarmed each time you grasp his legs, spend a few days reinforcing his trust. Forget the tricks for a while and hold him upside down in your arms while sitting on the floor. Scratch his tummy, and play with his feet. Repeat these procedures several times a day until you can manipulate his body at will.

Repeat the trick four or five times until he gets the feel for what he is supposed to do. You should continue with daily repetitions until he's doing the trick smoothly every time.

Shake

This is hardly a trick, since most dogs will come to their owners several times a day and extend a paw of friendship. In case Dandy hasn't already started it, you can teach this trick in an afternoon.

1. Begin the lesson while sitting in a chair. Call Dandy to you and have him sit on the floor facing you.

2. Extend your right hand toward him while holding a little tidbit in your left hand slightly above the level of his eyes. The sight of this tasty morsel immediately in front of his face will encourage him to remain in a sitting position.

3. Give the command *Shake,* and immediately pick up his right foot in your right hand, praise him with "Good dog," and immediately give him the tidbit.

4. Hold his paw for a second, then let it drop. Repeat this several times, then go outside and play catch or take him for a walk. Later in the day, call him to you and repeat the drill.

Canine Good Citizen

As the title implies, the holder of a Canine Good Citizen Certificate is well mannered and trained to react to certain situations with decorum and obedience. In other words, Dandy is a valued pet, not a problem.

Successful training, followed by a test given by a local AKC dog club will earn Dandy a certificate, which will tell the world that you care enough for your dog to devote the time to train him properly.

Good Citizen Test

This test is the only event sponsored or sanctioned by the AKC to include mixed-breed dogs. It requires a significant amount of your training time followed by an evaluation of Dandy's public behavior. This examination is not competitive; dogs are tested alone. Following AKC standards, dog clubs throughout the United States administer the test.

Dogs are evaluated in ten different activities. There are no points involved; the scoring is a simple pass or fail evaluation. Dogs are judged on essential, easily taught activities, which include the following exercises:

1. Accepting a Friendly Stranger: This exercise demonstrates your control of Dandy when he encounters a friendly person on the street or in your home. He is expected to allow the person to approach without displaying any aggression or resentment such as barking or growling.

In testing, the evaluator walks up to you and Dandy, stops, talks, and shakes hands with you, while ignoring Dandy. Dandy passes the test if he shows no signs of aggression or timidity, but keeps his position without going either to you or the evaluator.

Training in this case is quite simple. It only requires Dandy to be comfortable with strangers, which means you must exercise him in public places. You can teach him to sit or stand quietly by using positive control of his leash.

You need the help of several people with whom your new dog is not familiar. When one of your helpers approaches, tell Dandy to sit, then quietly step on his leash, holding him in place. Your helper greets you, shakes your hand and converses with you for a few seconds, then moves on. Dandy is rewarded if he has remained calmly in place.

If you begin this training while Dandy is a pup, he will never be shy of friends you meet on the street. If you are consistent in controlling him in place, he will never try to bounce around or jump up on your friends.

2. Sitting Politely for Petting: This test demonstrates the behavior of a trusting dog. Have Dandy sit beside you. You may use a *sit-stay* command if he has mastered that phase of obedience training. If not, refer to the obedience section of this book and review the training method described (see pages 79 to 84).

Once Dandy is in the sitting position, the evaluator will approach and

Canine Good Citizen certification is more difficult than it appears.

Poor manners can be avoided by early training.

pet his head and body, then circle you and your dog. During the evaluator's handling, you can talk to your pet, assuring him of your approval. To pass the test, Dandy must not show shyness or aggressiveness. He must passively allow petting in the manner previously described when you have put him in the sitting position.

Once again, the important part of training is to keep Dandy's focus or concentration on *you*, rather than on the evaluator. If he is looking at you, watching your hands, listening to your voice, he will have no trouble with this exercise. This is easily taught when Dandy is young; an adult dog will take a bit more time.

3. Appearance and Grooming: The evaluator will approach and inspect Dandy to determine if he is clean and well groomed, and has a healthy weight and appearance. The evaluator then lightly brushes or combs your dog, inspecting his ears and picking up each foot in turn. Dandy is allowed to sit or stand during this exercise, and you are expected to verbally assure him at all times.

This exercise is also best taught when Dandy is young. From the time you acquire him, ask your family members, dog-owning friends, and interested parties to participate. A well-mannered dog should be amenable to grooming by anyone when you are present.

4. Out for a Walk: Unlike heeling (page 83), Dandy may be on either side, but you must maintain leash control. You will find it easier to accomplish other exercises in this test if you always keep Dandy on your left. In the test, you will be given specific directions by the evaluator. You must turn left, right, reverse your direction, and stop, as instructed. You are allowed, even encouraged, to talk to Dandy as you proceed through this exercise.

5. Walking through a Crowd: This simple exercise is easily taught as soon as Dandy is leash trained. It requires him to walk on leash in a public place. The evaluator asks you to take him alongside at least three people, some of whom are accompanied by their dogs.

To pass the test, he can show natural interest in the dogs and their masters, but no aggressiveness or shyness. He shouldn't demonstrate lack of control by tugging at the leash, barking, or trying to play. You may talk to Dandy and encourage him during the exercise. Be sure to praise him when the two of you have passed the test.

Training for this phase of the test includes walking him on quiet streets of town, keeping his focus on you each time you meet someone, and under control by means of your voice and the leash. Progress to busier streets as time passes. You can ask help from several neighborhood friends. Have them stand around, perhaps with a well-behaved dog on a leash, as you take Dandy through this small crowd. If necessary, bait him with a treat when he shows interest in other dogs or people. Keep his interest focused on you by talking to him continuously.

6. *Sit* and *Down* on Command/ Staying in Place: This is an owner-control test with several parts. The first part of the test entails telling Dandy "sit," then giving the *down* command.

These commands are followed by the second part of the test, which is the *stay* command. Dandy is tested while wearing a 20-foot (6.1-m) leash (which never leaves your hand), and measures your influence on your dog while you walk away from him and return to his side.

The test is begun when you are instructed to put your dog in the *down* or *sit* position and tell him "stay." Gentle guidance may be used to encourage him to take the position, but most evaluators prefer that you don't touch your dog. You may not force Dandy or use food to cause him to assume the desired position. The evaluator then tells you to leave your dog. You walk the length of the 20-foot line and Dandy must stay in place, but may change positions. You are then instructed to return to your dog, take your former position beside him, and release him from the *stay.*

The *stay* is discussed fully on page 82, in the section on obedience training. Here, it differs from obedience commands in that you are allowed to encourage and guide Dandy into either of the two positions, and you maintain control through the long check line.

7. Coming When Called: This Good Citizen task exhibits the dog's obedience to coming to his owner when called. First tell Dandy "stay" or "wait," then leave him and walk 10 feet (3 m) away. Turn and face Dandy and call him. You may use encouragement such as patting your leg or motioning with your hands. The evaluator, meanwhile, may mildly distract Dandy by petting him. Training for this exercise is covered in the manners discussion on page 66.

8. Reaction to Another Dog: This exercise is a bit harder for puppies to accomplish and is a real test of their ability to focus on their handler. With Dandy on lead, walk across the floor or on the sidewalk. You meet a stranger who also has a polite, well-behaved dog on a leash. When you meet, you stop, exchange pleasantries, shake hands, and continue your stroll for another 5 yards (4.5 m). Dandy may show casual interest in the other dog, but must remain under your control. Dogs generally pass on the outside of their handlers, and usually the dog sits when you stop, but sitting is not mandatory. If you have trained Dandy to walk on your left, and the dog you meet is on its handler's left, the exercise is much smoother.

Training is similar to other exercises. Get and keep your dog's focus. Obtain the help of several friends with well-behaved dogs. Ask them to take their dogs, on leash, up and down the sidewalk or across the yard. They should keep their dogs on their left side while walking. As you approach your friend, gently tighten Dandy's leash a bit and softly speak to him. This will shift his concentration from the dog to you. Leash control is very important in this exercise, and a training collar should be used (see page 72 for discussion of training collars).

In the first phase of training, follow the previous directions and pass the friend and dog without stopping. Keep Dandy's lead snug, controlling his actions. Speak to your friend, who will return the greeting, and after passing them, reward Dandy according to his performance. If he only looked over his shoulder at the passing dog, he has made a good start and deserves a perfunctory

This Springer is learning to sit off lead.

reward. If he tugged at the lead, give him no reward. If he watched you, listening for commands, and hardly looked at either the person or dog, he should receive praise and perhaps a tidbit.

Repeat this training until Dandy passes dogs without a second thought. Then introduce the second phase, which is for you to stop and talk for a few seconds with the person, shake hands, and continue your walk. When you stop, it is an excellent idea (but not mandatory) to put Dandy in a *sit-stay* position.

9. Reacting to Distractions: This exercise tests Dandy's trust and confidence in you. Several distractions are commonly used. The evaluator selects a sound distraction such as the slamming or sudden opening of a door. Another noise is caused by dropping a book flat on the floor 10 or 12 feet (3 to 3.5 m) behind Dandy. The evaluator also may knock over a chair 6 or 8 feet (2 or 3 m) from Dandy or ask you to pass people who are engaged in loud talk and backslapping about 10 feet (3 m) from Dandy.

Another part of the test is a visual distraction. It may be a person on a bicycle who rides about 6 feet (2 m) from your dog, or someone pushing a rattling grocery cart passing about 10 feet (3 m) from Dandy. Other distractions might be someone running across your path or a person crossing your path on crutches, in a wheelchair, or using a walker.

In order to pass this test, Dandy may watch these happenings with natural curiosity, but he shouldn't panic, try to escape from them, bark, or show any aggressiveness or fear.

Training consists of conditioning by repeated exposure to these types of distractions. You can stage the sound distractions with the help of a friend. Expose Dandy to various sounds; include whistles and horns with those mentioned above. Keep his focus on you at all times. By your voice and tone, constantly let Dandy know he is safe. Control his actions with the lead. The sounds warrant his attention but should not be feared.

Visual distractions are best handled by walking Dandy on streets where cars, bicycles, skateboards, and motor scooters are zooming about. Keep him a significant distance from these distractions at first, then gradually change your path to bring him closer to the noises. Never put yourself or Dandy in danger. Later, when you feel he has excellent concentration on your voice and his leash, try walking through a supermarket parking lot. Remember, parking lots are dangerous places during busy hours.

If you ask, you will probably be allowed to take Dandy into a nursing home or care center where he will regularly meet people using wheelchairs, walkers, and crutches. This is also a fine place to teach him to sit for petting. Many elderly residents enjoy petting well-behaved dogs.

10. Supervised Separation: This exercise tests the ability of your dog to be left alone for three minutes without panic or showing excessive agitation. It is accomplished by putting Dandy on a 6-foot (2-m) lead. Hand the lead to the evaluator and leave Dandy's field of vision for three minutes.

Dandy will pass the test if he remains with the evaluator without chewing or tugging the lead, barking, pacing, or whining. He doesn't need to sit or lie down, and may move about, providing he remains calm and quiet. He should be interested in where you go, display mild agitation or nervousness, and be calmly anxious for your return.

Training for this exercise is easier if Dandy has been taught the *wait* command, as discussed under Crate Training (page 69). Tie him to a fence, tell him "wait," and walk around the house and out of sight. Repeat the command and exercise, each time telling him to wait, and gradually increasing the time you are away. It is very important for you to reward him with praise when he waits patiently for you. This task can be practiced in front of your home, in your backyard, or in any safe public place.

Obedience Overview

Obedience trials are competitions for AKC-registered dogs, but obedience training should be taught to every companion dog. Formal obedience work begins with the Novice level and progresses through the Companion Dog plane and finally to the Companion Dog Excellent and Utility levels.

Equipment

Just as you buy boots for hiking and dress shoes for special occasions, Dandy needs several different types of equipment in his wardrobe. For everyday wearing and when still a puppy, he needs a web or leather buckle collar and various types of leashes for different endeavors.

Choke (Training) Collar

A piece of equipment referred to previously, a training collar, commonly called a choke collar, should be used for obedience training. Choke collar is a misnomer if the collar is used correctly. It is a short length of smooth chain, a flat nylon tape, or strong nylon cord with a ring fastened to each end. In order to work as designed, it must be properly fitted to the dog; one size won't fit Dandy from puppy to adulthood. It should measure approximately 2 inches (5.1 cm) greater than the circumference of his neck. Most dogs respond equally well to either nylon or chain training collars.

Place the collar on Dandy so the end of the collar attached to the leash comes up the left side of the dog and crosses from left to right over the top of his neck. Keep Dandy on your left side, and when you need to correct his action, tighten the collar, then release it.

Leash (Lead)

For training, a short, lightweight leash is best. Use a 4-foot (1.2-m) web or leather lead that will comfortably reach from the dog to your hand. A lead shouldn't coil up in your hand or hang down to distract the dog. Later, our discussion will include various other leashes such as retractable leads and long check lines.

Fundamentals of Obedience Training

You can begin this training as soon as you are ready, but it should never become boringly repetitious. A young puppy has a short attention span—take care that training sessions never exceed it!

Command Clarity

Each command should be separated into five parts; each verbal part is enunciated clear and distinct in a crisp, normal tone. Dandy has better hearing than you do, so don't shout; it will distract from your effectiveness. A command shouldn't be repeated again and again for a single function. The tone for a command must be altogether different from the excited verbal praise you give when he performs correctly. The words of praise aren't as important as the eager manner and tone in which they are delivered. Here are examples:
• "Dandy" (hesitation)—he should respond by looking at you. Watch

his body language signals to be sure he is focusing on your voice. Allow a delay of a second or two, then give the command.

• "Come" (hesitate another few seconds).

• Enforce the action. Gently and firmly draw him to you by means of a long leash or check line.

• Release him from the command with "OK." He is now allowed to frisk around.

• Offer an appropriate reward. When reward is mentioned, it generally refers to a gentle "attaboy," or "good dog, Dandy," and some ear scratching.

Sit

With your puppy at your left side, in a calm, normal voice, say his name: "Dandy." Wait a second before you say "sit," and when you think the command is absorbed, push the pup's bottom to the ground.

Never use the term "sit down," because *sit* is one task, and *down* is an entirely different one. If he doesn't respond as you enforce the *sit* command, offer a small tidbit at eye level, immediately in front of and very close to his muzzle. This will encourage him to sit and hold that position. After a few seconds of sitting, release him by saying "OK," then reward him.

When Dandy doesn't perform the exercise correctly, don't make a big issue of the error; say "wrong" in a crisp, conversational tone, and make the necessary correction.

Practice the sitting exercise several times a day, but don't expect

When properly placed, training collars don't choke.

miracles; if you're lucky, he will catch on the first day, but don't count on it.

In the next session, practice the *sit* command several times, and if met with success, progress to another exercise. If it takes several daily sessions to learn to sit correctly, so be it.

Teaching a puppy to sit.

"Down" is a useful command to master.

Stay

This command is an extension of the previous one. When Dandy has mastered sitting, and is waiting for his reward, tell him "stay," while you remain standing at his right side. Present your flat, outstretched palm, fingers pointing toward the ground, in front of his muzzle as you give the *stay* command. If he tries to lie down or stand up, say "wrong," repeat the *stay* command, and put him into a sitting position again. After a few seconds of staying, release him from the stay with "OK," and give him his reward. Again, the command is broken into several parts: first, the dog's name, then the command, then the action, the release, and finally, the reward.

The next step is to move away from Dandy while he is obeying the *stay* command. When you put the leash on the ground and start to walk away, the faithful pup will try to follow. In a conversational voice, say "wrong," repeat the *stay* command, place Dandy in the sitting position, display your outstretched flat palm, and back away again. After a few tries, the pup will get the idea and stay put while you take several steps backward, then return quickly to his side, take your position with Dandy on your left, pick up the leash, and release him from the *stay*.

You must have Dandy's trust before this exercise will work. He must be focused on you and your action. He must realize that you will return and he will be rewarded upon your return. If he is concentrating on you, the other dogs sitting or lying nearby won't distract him.

Down

This command is used in obedience trials, and is also a convenient way to let the pup relax while you talk to neighbors on your daily walks. Give the command "Dandy (hesitation), down." Don't muddy the issue with extra words; never tell him to "lie down."

After you have given the *down* command, push his body to the ground slowly and gently. Don't fight him. When you need to encourage him to lie down, you may hold a tidbit so low that he can't reach it without lying down. Sometimes it's better to push his posterior into a sitting position and fold his elbows, placing his belly against the ground.

Once he has mastered the *down* command, tell him "stay" and back away a few steps while he is in the *down* position. Finish the exercise by returning to him, releasing him from the exercise, and lauding great praise upon him. Once the pup has confidence in your return, and that you will give him more praise and a tidbit, he will be happy to cooperate.

Heel

Dandy is now familiar with the training collar and leash, and doesn't panic when you occasionally tighten it. Each time you bring out his leash, he should be excited and realize that a walk is on the morning's agenda and new vistas are about to be discovered.

Heeling is another obedience exercise all well-behaved dogs should learn. Place Dandy on your left side, running the leash through your left hand, holding it with your right. Give the command "Dandy, sit," then, as you step off with your left foot, tell him "heel." As you walk along, keep his nose even with your thigh with gentle pressure on the leash.

If he continually wants to lag behind, you can encourage him to keep up by teasing him along with a tidbit held in your right hand. Soon Dandy will be walking by your side, taking turns and stops in his stride.

Talk to your heeling dog. Let him know he is doing what you want, tell

Heeling is not natural and more difficult to teach.

him "attaboy" when he is walking in the proper position. If you have had to correct him by tightening his leash, let him know he is doing OK now.

After he has properly heeled for a dozen steps, stop, and push his bottom to the ground to the sitting position as you tell him "sit." Then release him by saying "OK," reward with praise if he has performed satisfactorily, and begin the exercise all over again.

Heeling is a necessary part of obedience training and is used when going to and from the ring in dog shows. It's great when you need to maintain control of your companion in a crowd, and it's essential when crossing busy streets. That's where heeling should end; it's boring for Dandy, and although all dogs should learn to heel, they should be given more freedom whenever the situation and space will allow.

Formal Obedience Training

The Long Stay *Winner.*

If Dandy happens to be a pure-bred and you want to continue in obedience training and competition, contact a local dog club and express your interest. Join the club and participate in training classes. Only by training together with dozens of other dogs can you hope to compete in formal obedience classes. The fundamentals previously discussed are only the beginning if you and your dog have interest. Obedience classes include these simple exercises, continue through more complex and challenging tasks, and into tracking. Nothing is more rewarding than participating with your companion in advanced obedience work.

Chapter Seven

Emergencies

Life-threatening situations are rarely seen in dogs that are confined to a yard. When the security of a fence is forsaken, and Daisy is exploring the great outdoors off lead, a multitude of emergency situations may arise.

First Aid Kit

Today, one of the most important components of a first aid kit is a cellular telephone. If you have one, take it along; it provides an immediate means of contacting your veterinarian and may save Daisy's life. Write the veterinarian's number on your first aid kit, and if you have an emergency, tell the receptionist what has happened, that you're on your way to the hospital, and the approximate time you expect to arrive.

Evaluate the Emergency

Speed is important when evaluating an emergency; you must be ready to take some calculated action immediately. To prepare for emergencies, you should attend canine first aid classes when Daisy is a pup. You should know how to administer canine CPR (see page 88), how to muzzle your dog, apply pressure bandages or tourniquets, and the proper way to carry her.

You should be familiar with your dog's normal respiratory rate and character, pulse rate, mucous membrane color, body temperature, capillary filling time, and other vital signs. Knowing the normal allows

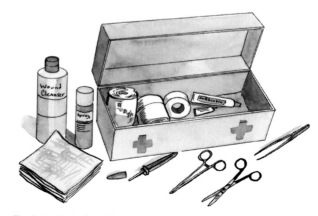

Tools to include in first aid kit.

Small Nylon Belt-Pouch First Aid Kit

- Artificial tears
- Bandage scissors
- Disinfectant soap
- 4-foot (1.2-m) length of soft cotton rope for muzzle
- 3 percent hydrogen peroxide
- Pad and pencil
- Roll of 1-inch (2.5-cm) adhesive tape
- Roll of 3-inch (7.6-cm) gauze bandage
- Rubber tube for a tourniquet
- Styptic stick
- Thermometer, electronic or mercury, rectal
- Triple antibiotic cream
- Tweezers or inexpensive hemostatic forceps
- Vital signs chart

you to quickly recognize and evaluate the abnormal.

Before you venture abroad on long walks, take time to record your dog's normal vital signs. Don't try to remember these values; write them down! A sample chart is furnished on page 87; put such a chart in your first aid kit.

Temperature and Respiration

With a glass or digital thermometer, take and record her rectal temperature early one morning, and again after she has been playing hard. The normal range is from 101.5 to 102.5°F (38.5 to 39.5°C). What is Daisy's temperature?

Similarly, before and after exercise, record her respiratory rate and the character of her breathing; see if it is shallow or labored. A dog's normal respiration rate is between 10 and 30 breaths per minute, and can only be evaluated when she is breathing through her nose, not while she is panting. What is Daisy's rate and character?

While resting, and again after playing, take and record her pulse by pressing your finger against the inside of her thigh, about halfway between her stifle and hip. An alternative way to check the heart rate is to firmly press the chest wall with your hand at the level of her elbow. A dog's normal resting heart rate is between 70 and 90 beats per minute. What is Daisy's? Does it increase with exercise?

Capillary Filling Time

Observe your dog's oral mucous membranes; the color of her tongue and gums should be a bright, moist shade of pink. Now press your finger tightly against her gums for a few seconds. The tissue will turn white under your finger, and as you remove your finger, it will quickly return to its normal color. Check the time the white area takes to reach the normal pink color. This simple test is called *capillary filling time*, which should be about two seconds. What is Daisy's capillary filling time?

Eyes

Observe her eyes. They should be bright, moist, and glossy, with crystal clear corneas.

These normal values will be invaluable if you meet with an accident and need to report her vital signs to Daisy's doctor.

Treating Emergencies

Sudden illness or injury is frightening to a dog and Daisy needs reassurance just as a frightened, injured person does. Keep your voice calm; speak in low, soothing tones. Gently touch Daisy's head, pet her and make her aware that you are trying to help her.

Car Accidents

Car accidents are among the worst nightmares you might expect to encounter. When a dog has been hit by an automobile, an emergency exists, regardless of where it occurs or how it happened. Accident victims require professional help as quickly as possible! If a car hits Daisy, you must act quickly to determine whether your best course is an immediate trip to the veterinarian, or if she should be treated at the accident site to control hemorrhaging.

If necessary, control any visible hemorrhaging, then wrap her up. Keep her quiet and warm. On your

Normal Values

Pulse rate	70 to 90 per minute
Pulse quality	Strong and steady
Temperature	101.5°F or 38.5°C
Respiration	10 to 30 per minute
Respiratory character	Even and deep
Mucous membrane	Bright pink; moist
Capillary filling time	2 seconds
Eye appearance	Bright; corneas clear and moist

My Dog's Normal Values

Before exercise   *After exercise*

_____	Pulse rate	_____
_____	Pulse quality	_____
_____	Temperature	_____
_____	Respiratory rate	_____
_____	Respiratory character	_____
_____	Mucous membrane	_____
_____	Capillary filling time	_____
_____	Eye appearance	_____

Correct CPR technique.

weak and staggering, overheated or shivery cold.

Signs of shock include pale or bluish gums and tongue, lengthy capillary filling time, rapid, shallow respiration, a weak, thready pulse, and a rapid heart rate of usually more than 150 beats per minute. These signs are variable according to the extent of the shock.

Causes of shock are also quite variable. Shock may be the result of any incident causing internal or external hemorrhaging, or severe trauma. Other causes include twisted stomach (see page 110 for a discussion of gastric torsion), severe animal bites, poisons, deep puncture wounds, snakebite, and serious illnesses. Shock has been seen in cases of allergic reaction to antibiotics and other drugs as well.

Shock is relative, and may be progressive. When it is suspected, control the bleeding, keep the patient warm, and get the patient to a veterinarian quickly.

way to the veterinarian's office, use your cellular phone to report her vital signs. If she is exhibiting pain, muzzle her before handling. Use a board, jacket, or blanket as a stretcher on which to transport Daisy. Time is of the essence!

A car accident might result in shock, fractures, lacerations, and hemorrhage. Of those, shock is the most perplexing.

Recognizing Shock

Shock is a difficult syndrome to define, evaluate, and treat. It is not a simple entity, but a complex multi-symptom condition, one for which you must always be on the alert when emergencies arise. Dogs in shock don't always have the same signs; they may be prostrate or relatively alert, tense and anxious or

CPR

CPR or cardiopulmonary resuscitation should be used if a dog's heart has stopped. The technique is as follows: Lay Daisy on her right side, and with the heel of your hand, press downward to compress her ribs and chest immediately behind her elbow for a second, then release. Continue this intermittent manual cardiac pressure until her heart begins to beat on its own. If no heartbeat is noted after a few minutes, discontinue, wait for a few seconds, and if you feel no beating, continue the cardiac massage.

Artificial Respiration

Clear the dog's mouth of mucus and debris. Tilt her head back, hold her mouth shut with your hand, and place your mouth over her muzzle. Blow into the dog's nose until you see her chest begin to expand. Release your hand and allow her to exhale, and repeat the procedure every five seconds.

Pressure Bandage

If Daisy is bleeding profusely, locate the source of the spurting blood and apply a bandage. The bandage must exert sufficient pressure to stop the hemorrhage and should be placed directly over the source of bleeding. Tie or tape the bandage securely in place and keep Daisy quiet. Get a blanket or use your jacket as a stretcher to carry the injured dog. In order to prevent further damage, it's important to handle her gently and minimally.

Muzzle

Even the most gentle pet may snap or bite viciously when she is frightened, in pain, suffering from shock, or feels threatened. Approach Daisy slowly, lower yourself to her level, and speak to her in a soft, calm voice. Avoid direct eye contact with her, and if she shows apprehension or aggression, apply a muzzle before you go any further. Remember, time is important, and you can't help her if you can't examine and handle her.

To form a muzzle, tie a single, loose knot in the center of the length of cord and slip the loop over her closed jaws. Snug the knot on top of her muzzle as far back as possible, put the ends of the cord beneath her lower jaw, and tie another single knot. Then take the ends of the cord behind her ears and tie it snugly in a slipknot. If you don't have a muzzle cord in your first aid kit, tear a strip of gauze about 4 feet (1.2 m) long from a bandage roll and substitute it for the cord.

Skin Lacerations

If Daisy steps on a broken bottle or sharp tin can, or runs into a pointed stick, examine her injuries. If the wound is extensive or is bleeding profusely, immediately apply a pressure bandage and get her to a veterinarian. If the injury is nothing more than a minor scratch or tiny skin tear, trim the hair away from the wound with scissors, clean with an antiseptic soap, and apply a triple antibiotic cream.

Pad Injuries

Lacerations or punctures involving only the pad leather may not require veterinary care but should be bandaged to prevent contamination. After cleaning and the application of antibiotic cream, place a snug but nonrestrictive bandage over the wounded pad and tape it in place.

Extensive Lacerations and Punctures

In case a laceration is extensive, or a puncture extends into the muscle and is bleeding profusely, control the hemorrhage with a pressure bandage or apply finger pressure. Ask a friend to bring your car to the dog, if possible; if not, carry her to the car. Don't allow her to walk back to your vehicle, even if she is willing to do so. Get Daisy to the veterinarian.

Stick and Nail Punctures

If the stick has broken off and remains in the dog's tissues, leave it alone. Carry her to your car and transport her to your veterinarian. If you attempt to remove the stick, you might cause increased hemorrhaging or you could leave a tiny piece of the stick lodged deep in the tissues where it is difficult to locate.

If you don't know the cause of the puncture, watch for bleeding, and apply a pressure bandage if needed. An immediate visit to the veterinarian is indicated in the case of any deep puncture. Always assume that such a puncture has a foreign body such as a wood fragment retained within it. Every puncture has a potential infection associated with it and your veterinarian should explore the wound and prescribe treatment as soon as possible. Ask your veterinarian about the administration of tetanus antitoxin.

Fractures

Broken bones are cause for alarm, but require careful planning and emergency treatment. In general, no emergency splinting techniques should be used. The dog should be carefully restrained, and taken to the veterinarian.

There are many types of fractures: simple, greenstick, compound, and comminuted.

Simple fractures are those not associated with a skin tear.

Greenstick fractures are incomplete breaks in which the bone ends are held in place by the fibrous covering of the bone.

Compound fractures are those in which the broken bone ends are exposed to the outside through skin wounds, and should always be considered contaminated. Don't medicate the open wounds or touch the bone unless necessary.

Comminuted fractures are multiple breaks, or crushed bone.

In all cases of fractures, evaluate shock, control hemorrhaging, and transport the dog to the veterinarian as quickly as possible. Carry her on a board or makeshift stretcher, if possible, and minimize movement of the fracture.

Ear Lacerations

Dog fights and other traumatic encounters may result in a torn

Always incorporate a bit of hair in the tape to keep bandage from slippling.

earflap. When such a laceration occurs, bleeding will be profuse, and will be made worse by constant head shaking. Steady Daisy and bandage the torn ear snuggly to the side of her head with gauze. Wrap the gauze with tape, overlapping the bandage and extending the tape onto the hair of her cheek. Although less serious than other wounds, bandaging ears will save blood spatters on your clothing and car while on the trip to the veterinarian.

Nose Bleeds

This emergency is usually caused by a sharp blow to the tip of the muzzle. If the hemorrhage is minimal, keeping Daisy quiet for half an hour is likely all the treatment needed. If you see more copious bleeding, apply cold packs to her muzzle for several minutes and keep her quite still for half an hour after the bleeding stops. If the bleeding is spontaneous and not associated with any trauma, keep her quiet and call your veterinarian.

Tourniquet

A tourniquet is a last resort for hemorrhage control and should be used only when there is no other way to stop a bleeding wound. Use the rubber tube from your kit or fashion a tourniquet from a strip of gauze, a shoelace, necktie, or any similar ropelike fabric. Properly placed, a tourniquet stops the flow of arterial blood from the heart to the injured part of the body. If a foot is torn, the tourniquet is placed just above the ankle. If the wound is located on the trunk of the body, the head, or upper leg, a tourniquet can't be used, and a pressure bandage or finger pressure should be used to stop the hemorrhage.

If you use a tourniquet, tighten it only enough to stop the hemorrhage and release it for a few seconds every 15 minutes.

Poisoning

If evidence indicates that Daisy has been poisoned, take her vital signs, then call your veterinarian. If you can locate some of the poisonous agent, or a label from the container, take it to the veterinarian. If the label instructs you to induce vomiting, you can do so by placing about a teaspoonful of salt on the back of the dog's tongue. A tablespoonful of hydrogen peroxide may be administered orally to also produce vomiting. Syrup of ipecac may be used, but it frequently is slow to work.

Urinary Blockage

Characteristically, the dog repeatedly will stand and strain, passing only a drop or two of urine. He may cry while attempting to urinate, and will usually squat instead of raising his hind leg.

Urinary blockage is caused by stones that form in the urinary bladder, pass down the urethra, and lodge over the penis. They block the passage of urine to some degree, sometimes completely. When you see this problem, take the dog to your veterinarian immediately.

Chapter Eight

Diseases and Illnesses

Choosing a Good Veterinarian

Dandy deserves a good veterinarian, a doctor who is competent, knowledgeable, communicative, and available to discuss Dandy's needs. This professional should provide advice about routine care and preventive medicine, as well as prescribing treatment for any illnesses and emergencies. The veterinarian is a resource that you cannot do without. How do you choose a *good veterinarian*?

• Seek references from your friends, then call for an appointment with the veterinarian before you acquire a dog. If you're new in a community or don't know anyone who uses a veterinarian, browse the yellow pages. Remember this: The magnitude of the advertisement may be inversely proportional to the skill of the doctor. When you call, reliable professionals will give you a few minutes of their time and will welcome your visit and your inquiries.

• Don't waste the veterinarian's time or yours; make a list of questions to ask, and stay with your script.

• Ask how off-hours emergencies are handled. If the veterinarian does not provide off-hours treatment and refers such calls to an emergency care clinic, check out that clinic as well.

• Ask to take a tour of the animal hospital at a convenient time. Observe the available facilities and equipment, the cleanliness and organization of the hospital.

• Choose a doctor who is friendly, caring, and knowledgeable, and whose technical staff is helpful and ready to share their knowledge with you. Explain your animal health care needs, and see how the veterinarian responds to them.

• Communication is the key to a good relationship with your veterinarian, so find a clinician who is willing to listen to you.

• Check the cost of spaying your female, or castrating your male. Obtain a fee schedule or inquire about fees for routine office visit examinations, vaccinations, fecal exams, and worm treatment. Ask about heartworm, flea, and tick preventive plans and their cost.

It's important to let this professional know that you are placing your trust in him or her, and that you don't take this relationship lightly. The professional should realize that he or she is sharing the stewardship of a pet with you; you are on the same team.

If the veterinarian resists being interviewed or doesn't seem to share your concern about reliable, effective preventive care, you are in the wrong hospital. A veterinarian who has no time for you as a prospective dog owner and client will probably have little time for you after you have obtained a pet.

Once you have acquired your new dog, check out the doctor's

Preventive medicine begins with vaccinations.

tableside manners. Is the veterinarian gentle and thorough when examining Dandy? Is time available for a bit of small talk and a quick rub of Daisy's chin?

Questions to Ask Your New Veterinarian
- Do you take emergency off-hours calls?
- If not, to whom are they referred?
- What are your office hours?
- Are appointments required, and if so, how far in advance?
- May I schedule a tour of your hospital?
- Do you have diagnostic laboratory facilities on premises?
- Do you have X-ray and ultrasound equipment?
- Are you equipped for gastroscopic exams?
- What are your paying or billing requirements?
- Do you accept credit cards?
- Do you recommend pet insurance?
- Do you publish a fee schedule?
- If not, what is the cost of an office call?
- How much will you charge to spay (castrate) my dog?
- What is the average cost for external parasite control?
- What vaccination procedures do you use?
- How often should I have my dog checked for worms?

The Life Expectancy of Dogs

If your new dog is a puppy, you should expect to share your life with him for 12 to 15 years. Small dogs, the size of a Cocker Spaniel, usually live longer than their giant counterparts. Terriers are known for particularly long lives. Nutrition, preventive medicine, and health care influence the life expectancy of dogs, as does the amount and quality of exercise they are provided.

Signs of Puppy Ailments

No matter how well you treat your new dog, Dandy will undoubtedly get sick at some time. Usually, puppy ailments are simple, uncomplicated illnesses, and quick recovery can be expected. Signs of these ailments that persist should alert you to more serious diseases. If you do not see a quick recovery, consult your veterinarian.

Diarrhea

Liquid stool is not actually a disease; it is a sign or symptom of some intestinal irritation (see gastritis and enteritis on page 110). It is probably the most common problem seen in puppies and is often the result of overeating or eating the wrong foods. Milk, other rich foods, or table scraps are often to blame.

Dandy may continue eating and playing normally, but his bowel control is not what you might desire, and his feces are watery, and often foul-smelling.

When you first notice diarrhea, withhold all food immediately. Let his stomach rest for 12 hours, during which time he should be kept confined for observation. A small pen in the yard or a bathroom with the floor covered with newspapers will do. During his confinement, you should watch for lethargy, vomiting, blood in his stool, or other signs of serious illness.

If Dandy shows none of these signs, start him on a diet of 1 part cooked rice; 1 part dry, fat-free cottage cheese; and 1 part cooked and drained hamburger. Mix these ingredients together and give him about one-third the total quantity of food he is accustomed to, divided into three meals. Feed him no other food for at least two days.

If his problem is simply from eating something indigestible, a day or two of this bland diet should be sufficient. While on the bland diet, if you can manage it, administer orally either kaopectate or bismuth subsalicylate (Pepto Bismol) three times daily. Call your veterinarian to obtain specific dosages for your dog's size.

If the diarrhea persists, is bloody, or is accompanied by vomiting, take him to the veterinarian.

Vomiting

Regurgitation or vomiting is likewise not a disease, but the sign or symptom of a disease. Eating foreign material such as leaves, sticks, bones, pieces of toys, grass, or rocks may cause vomiting. Confinement is a necessary part of treatment. Withhold all food and water for 24 hours and watch for blood in the vomit, or accompanying diarrhea. *Give nothing orally to a vomiting dog.* If the vomiting has subsided or stopped in four hours, allow Dandy to lick a couple of ice cubes and watch him closely. If vomiting doesn't resume, administer a spoonful of bismuth subsalicylate three times daily. After a 24-hour fast, begin the aforementioned bland diet concurrently with the oral medication.

If Dandy's vomit contains bits of sponge rubber, shreds of steel wool, or any other obvious foreign material, get him to a veterinarian quickly.

Blood in his vomit or persistent vomiting may be a sign of serious systemic disease and shouldn't be neglected for even a day.

Scratching

If he is like most puppies, Dandy will occasionally scratch at his body. If the scratching is intermittent and infrequent, it can be ignored, but if it is persistent, it may be a sign of flea infestation, mange mites, dry skin, allergy, or other disease, and should merit a trip to your veterinarian.

Scratching at an ear might be evidence of ear mites or an ear infection. Biting at the skin just above his tail may indicate overfull or impacted anal sacs, and nibbling at one foot could be caused by a burr caught between his toes.

It's easier to hide the pill in peanut butter.

Appropriate treatment depends on the cause of Dandy's scratching. If this cause is apparent, as in the case of a burr, gently pluck it out, or if you see fleas, buy a bottle of flea shampoo labeled for use on dogs of Dandy's age and use it. Of course, destroying the fleas on his body is the solution for only a minor part of the problem. Flea control is discussed later in this chapter, beginning on page 99.

If Dandy's scratching is caused by invisible causes, your veterinarian will be able to diagnose it and prescribe treatment.

Hair Loss

Often seen around the face of new puppies, this patchy hairless appearance may be caused by mange mites or a multitude of other conditions. All hair loss should be evaluated by your veterinarian.

Preventive Health Care: Vaccinations

Most breeders begin a series of vaccinations soon after puppies are weaned, and annual booster vaccinations should be continued throughout the dog's life. Dandy's particular vaccination schedule should be designed for him and his lifestyle. The following discussion relates to contagious diseases that may be prevented by appropriate vaccinations.

Canine Distemper (CD)

In spite of available vaccines, canine distemper (dog plague or hard pad) continues to be a significant threat to young puppies. It is caused by a virus that attacks the dog's respiratory tract, intestinal tract, and brain. Often resulting in twitching, convulsions, and death, the reservoir for CD exists in stray dog populations and wild carnivores such as raccoons, foxes, and minks.

Small puppies may suddenly die from CD with few visible symptoms. Older dogs may show fever, loss of appetite, lethargy, dehydration, diarrhea, and vomiting. A yellow or green ocular discharge often accompanies CD, and coughing is another common sign of the disease. A few dogs seem to respond to various treatments, only to die

later from convulsions and paralysis. Hardened footpads, tooth enamel deficiencies, and permanent neurological signs such as blindness or twitching of extremities often affect those dogs that miraculously survive the disease.

Don't neglect your puppy's vaccinations! The first of a series of CD vaccinations is given at weaning time, and may be combined with other vaccines. To maintain a protective level of immunity, annual boosters are required. Keep Dandy confined and away from any possible exposure until he has had at least his first two vaccinations.

Infectious Canine Hepatitis (ICH or CAV-1)

This disease is a contagious, incurable, systemic disease causing fatal damage to the liver. It is highly communicable among dogs, but is not contagious to humans. CAV-1 is an abbreviation for the causative organism, canine adenovirus, type 1. Symptoms often mimic those of distemper, including sudden death in young pups.

Vaccines are highly effective in preventing ICH and are usually combined with other immunizing agents at weaning time, with annual boosters required.

Leptospirosis

Usually shortened to Lepto, this disease causes a sometimes fatal kidney damage. The causative organism is a *spirochete* organism, similar to a bacterium. Highly contagious, the Lepto organism is transmitted by urine and can infect humans as well as other animals.

Signs of Lepto infection include lethargy, lack of appetite, thirst, rusty-colored urine, diarrhea, and vomiting. Affected dogs sometimes walk with a peculiar stilted, roach-backed gait. Antibiotic treatment may be effective, but permanent kidney damage often results from an infection. Leptospirosis vaccine is usually combined with CD and CAV-1 immunizing products at weaning time, and is repeated annually.

Parvo and Corona Viruses

These two are among the more recently discovered viruses causing often fatal canine diseases. Both diseases typically produce severe diarrhea, vomiting, dehydration, and depression. Spread by saliva, feces, vomit, or one-on-one contact with affected dogs, these diseases are particularly devastating to young puppies. Humans are not susceptible to these viruses, but they may inadvertently transmit the causative virus on shoes or clothes.

Vaccinations are usually given at weaning age with annual boosters required. Consult with your veterinarian about the use of these products.

Kennel Cough

This syndrome is caused by a number of different viruses and bacteria. *Parainfluenza* virus and *Bordetella* bacteria produce the typical coughing, fever, loss of appetite, and depression. This syndrome affects dogs of all ages, is quite contagious, and is easily spread by aerosol (airborne droplets of saliva and nasal discharge from an affected dog's cough or sneeze). The bronchial tubes, trachea, and larynx are affected. Uncomplicated kennel cough may bother the dog and owner for two or three weeks if the dog is not stressed. It has a much lower fatality rate than some of the diseases discussed previously, but when complicated by pneumonia or other problems, it may be serious.

Upper respiratory disease vaccines include intranasal types that are often less predictable than injectable types, but their reliability is improving. Consult with your veterinarian about the best product to protect Dandy.

Lyme Disease

The vector or carrier of this disease of dogs and humans is the deer tick. A few years ago, Lyme disease was more commonly reported in the northeastern and midwestern regions of the United States, but it has now spread nationwide, and is presently known to exist in at least 40 states. White-tailed deer and field mice are the principal reservoir hosts for the Lyme virus.

Lyme disease may cause lameness in an affected dog and is accompanied by heat, pain, and swelling of one or more leg joints. Body temperature is usually elevated and the dog is listless. Early treatment is important to be effective.

The risk of Lyme disease is related to the length of time an infected tick is attached to your dog. When you are in an area where deer ticks have been seen, check your dog at least once daily for their presence. They are tiny (about 0.1 inch or .04 cm in diameter), black, or red and black, and resemble a little mole on the skin. As they suck blood, they grow much larger and grayer, with the female ticks sometimes reaching the size of a grape. Follow the directions on page 101 for tick removal.

There is a Lyme disease vaccine available but its efficacy is debatable; check with Dandy's veterinarian. Newer vaccines against Lyme disease are being developed and may soon be available. A good tick-preventive program is essential in any case.

Rabies

Rabies, a fatal viral disease of all warm-blooded animals including dogs and humans is spread primarily by contact with the saliva of an infected animal. It is usually associated with bite wounds.

Brain changes are the characteristic signs of rabies. The average time lapse between an infected bite and signs of the disease (incubation period) can be as short as two or three weeks but occasionally it is several months. The rabies virus travels from the site of the bite to the brain by way of nerve trunks; therefore, if the infecting bite occurs on a foot, it results in a longer incubation period. After reaching the brain, the rabies virus migrates to the salivary glands where it reproduces, causing typical signs.

The signs of rabies in a dog are varied. Sometimes the affected dog becomes aggressive and highly irritable. As the disease progresses, the dog may become partially paralyzed (dumb rabies) or vicious (furious rabies).

Immunization for this important disease is usually administered later than other vaccines. Check with your veterinarian for local requirements. Many cities and counties have laws requiring rabies vaccinations when dogs reach three months of age, and the law usually stipulates that the vaccine must be administered by, or under the direction of, licensed and USDA-accredited veterinarians.

Reservoirs for rabies virus are found in wild animals such as skunks, foxes, raccoons, coyotes, bats, and other wildlife. Since this incurable and fatal disease can infect all warm-blooded animals, great emphasis is placed on rabies preventive programs.

Parasites

Parasites are living organisms that derive their nutrition and live at the expense of their hosts. Some parasites are visible little bugs; others are fungus plants.

External Parasites (Ectoparasites)

Parasites that live on the outside of your dog are many and varied.

Ranging from microscopic fungi and mites to ticks the size of grapes, they are all harmful to Dandy's health.

Ringworm and Mange: Ringworm is not caused by a worm, but a tiny fungus that rarely takes the shape of a ring. Mange is caused by several different mites, each of which is treated differently. These microscopic parasites cause infestations that may result in hair loss, itching, irritation, and redness.

The most common mange mites are *Cheyletiella, Demodex, Psoroptes*, and *Sarcoptes*.

Allergies, nutritional problems, hormonal imbalances, and physical irritations may also cause skin irritation and hair loss. These conditions are commonly mistaken for parasitism and are often mistreated. Skin scrapings must be examined under a microscope to identify mites responsible for mange lesions. Skin scrapings, ultraviolet light, or cultures are used to identify fungal infections.

Don't rely on a universal mange dip or ringworm salve to cure skin diseases. Those products may create new problems while doing nothing toward solving the initial one. When you discover a hair loss or surface irritation, invest in a trip to your veterinarian.

Ear Mites: Another mite, *Otodectes*, may parasitize ear canals of both cats and dogs. It is large enough to be seen with a magnifying glass and lives inside the pet's ear canals. Ear mites cause severe irritation, and result in the dog scratching at its ears. Ear canals usually fill with a dark wax. If Dandy's ears are bothering him, look for the excessive wax, and take him to the veterinarian. Treatment usually consists of cleaning the ears thoroughly and the application of mite-killing medication into the ear canals.

Lice: *Pediculosis* is the term used to describe a louse infestation. These parasites may be of the sucking or biting varieties, and are easily diagnosed and treated. All life stages of the louse live on the dog, and topical treatments such as dips or medicated baths are usually satisfactory therapy.

Diagnosis is made by discovering tiny white nits or louse eggs stuck to hairs on Dandy's back, often near his rump. The adult lice are easily seen scurrying about on his skin, causing him to scratch when they bite or bury their heads to suck blood.

When you are sure of the diagnosis, buy a powder or shampoo containing safe insecticides and use it. Plant derivative insecticides such as pyrethrins may be effective and are always worth a try. Lice may spread to other dogs in the household, so it is usually best to treat them as well.

Fleas: Probably the most irritating ectoparasite is also the most common one. The diminutive flea is seen in backyard or kenneled dogs, and heavier infestations are found on dogs living in warmer, more humid climates. Cat fleas are found quite commonly on dogs.

This parasite lives part of its life cycle off the dog, and is therefore

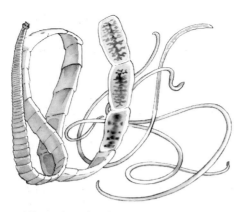

Life cycles of major ectoparasites.

difficult to treat definitively. Fleas cause other problems; they are secondary hosts for tapeworms and the fleas' saliva can cause allergy in dogs that is confusing to diagnose and difficult to treat.

Fleas bite the dog, making small wounds in the skin, then lap the blood as it oozes from the wound. Adult fleas can leap great distances; sometimes they land on humans.

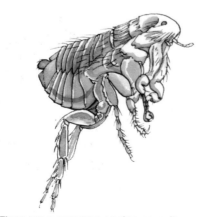

Fleas are a common canine parasite.

They aren't particular where they receive their blood meal, but will usually be found on a dog or cat when one is available.

A fine-toothed comb may be used to locate fleas. Carefully run it through Dandy's coat over the region of his pelvis. The parasites will be caught between the flea comb's teeth, or will jump from his hair in front of the comb. If you don't find adult fleas, you may see some of their excreta (feces), which appear as tiny, black, comma-shaped debris.

Fleas are quite irritating to the dog, whether or not they cause an allergy. They are often responsible for Dandy's licking, chewing, and scratching, and the formation of hot spots, another skin condition.

A part-time resident on the dog, the flea arrives on its host, feeds, mates, and lays eggs. The eggs are deposited on the dog, and fall off in the doghouse or on your carpet. The eggs hatch into larvae that feed on dandruff and other organic debris. The larvae pupate, adults emerge, and begin looking for a host. The adult flea can live for more than 100 days without a blood meal.

If a flea problem is identified, bring out the heavy artillery—don't take this infestation lightly! Vacuum the doghouse and your home, launder bedding, and treat the doghouse and your carpets with dog-safe flea killers:

• Borax powder is generally a safe product to use on dogs' bedding and carpets; it is nontoxic, killing fleas by dehydration.

• A premise spray or flea bomb may be used to rid the house of this parasite, but both can be quite dangerous unless all label directions are carefully followed.

• There are several new flea-repellent products available from your veterinarian. Some are in oral tablet form; others are in liquid form that is applied topically on Dandy's skin once a month. Some kill the flea eggs; others kill only the adult. Follow your veterinarian's advice about the products, their safety, cost, and effectiveness.

• New biological control programs are presently being initiated in some areas. One involves the yard application of tiny nematodes (worms) that consume flea eggs but are harmless to humans and pets. Others involve the use of insect growth regulators (IGR) that interfere with the flea's life cycle.

• A new generation of flea collars is also available that repels the parasites, rather than killing them after they cause their damage.

• Organic products such as pyrethrum and other natural insecticides are usually considered safer. That may or may not be the case, but they are less effective than the contemporary products.

• A collar is available that emits high frequency sounds to repel fleas, but its effectiveness is suspect.

Do not use oral medication, dips, sprays, powders, medicated collars, or other drugs that are not labeled for Dandy's specific age and weight. Don't use more than one product on Dandy at a time without approval by your veterinarian. Also be careful with the use of all systemic medications in a pregnant or lactating female.

Ticks: An adult tick buries its head in a dog's skin and sucks blood for several days. Male ticks are quite small, about the size of a pinhead; females often reach the size of a grape when they fill with blood. After a blood meal, females fall off, lay thousands of eggs, then die. Their other life stages may be completed on the dog (as in the brown dog tick), or they may use birds, deer, rodents, or other mammals for secondary hosts.

If you find a tick on Dandy, put on a pair of rubber gloves, and grasp it as close to the dog's skin as possible with a pair of tweezers or forceps. With firm steady traction, pull it out. Ticks often imbed themselves under

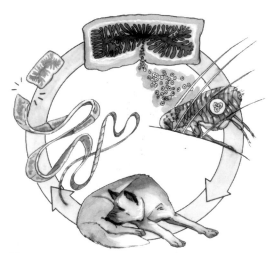

The tapeworm life cycle is complex and favors the parasite.

Dandy's collar, in the armpits, around the ears, and over the withers.

Don't panic if the tick's head breaks off. Contrary to popular belief, the imbedded part of the tick that remains in a dog shouldn't cause a serious problem; it may result in a minor local irritation but rarely a systemic infection. After the tick has been extracted, destroy it by placing it in alcohol. Don't try to drown a tick in water, don't squash it, and don't handle it with your bare fingers.

Once or twice daily, clean Dandy's skin with alcohol where the tick was embedded. This will keep the scab off and allow drainage from the wound left by the tick.

It's a common belief that ticks will be forced to detach if you heat their bodies with the flame of a match or the hot tip of a hair curling iron. Heat really doesn't hasten their exit and may be hazardous to your dog. Another old tick-removal technique is to place a drop of acetone, alcohol, or nail polish remover on the tick to make it back out quickly. The theory is that the rapid evaporation of such products cool the tick, causing it to release its hold. That idea has more credibility than heating the tick, but it doesn't work every time.

Tick-borne Diseases: Lyme disease was discussed under diseases preventable by vaccine (page 97).

Ehrlichiosis is another tick-borne disease to be reckoned with. It is transmitted by the brown dog tick, and is a serious disease, manifested by nosebleeds, swelling of the limbs, anemia, and a multitude of other signs. It can be fatal if not treated early.

Internal Parasites (Endoparasites)

These parasites live in a dog's intestinal tract, causing nutritional problems and physical irritation affecting the condition and attitude of the host. Parasites such as roundworms, hookworms, whipworms, coccidia, and tapeworms may seriously affect the general health and vitality of puppies.

Roundworms (Ascarid): Immature roundworms (larvae) may remain hidden in cysts in a female dog's tissues throughout her life. During pregnancy, these larvae migrate from their cysts into the unborn puppies' tissues. When the pup is born, the larvae migrate to its small intestine and mature. Adult roundworms lay eggs that pass out in the dog's feces, become sources of infestation for other dogs, and in certain rare instances, children. These and other parasite ova or eggs are identified by microscopic examination of puppies' feces.

The principal effect of roundworm infestation is a loss of condition of the host because the parasite competes with the puppy for food, and a heavy infestation of roundworms will nearly starve a pup to death. Typically, these malnourished dogs will be unthrifty, have a potbelly, and lack energy.

A stool sample from Dandy should be taken to your veterinarian at least once a year. If parasite ova are found in the stool sample, your veterinarian will prescribe an appropriate medication for treatment.

Hookworms: Ancylostoma, the canine hookworm, is a more serious parasite. This microscopic worm hatches from eggs passed in the stool of infected dogs. In addition to being spread through routes similar to the roundworm, the hookworm larvae are able to penetrate the skin of dogs, then migrate throughout the tissues, ending up in the small intestine. There, they attach to the lining of the gut and suck blood.

The principal sign of hookworms is anemia. The severity of blood loss depends on the degree of infestation. Puppies may die from heavy infestations of hookworms.

Diagnosis is made by microscopic examination of a fecal sample. Treatment is usually administered by a veterinarian, and follow-up fecal examinations are often scheduled.

Whipworms: *Trichuris* infestation is relatively rare. This parasite lives in the cecum, an outpouching of the large intestine. Causing chronic diarrhea, whipworm infestation is diagnosed by fecal examination, and treated with oral medication. Repeated stool examinations are usually advised to be sure this parasite is eliminated.

Coccidia: Coccidia are microscopic, protozoan parasites that live in the dog's intestine. Infestation usually causes chronic diarrhea, often with blood. It can be diagnosed by fecal examination and treatment with various medications

is usually successful, although not a sure thing. Repeated fecal examinations are usually recommended following treatment.

Tapeworms: These endoparasites require secondary hosts. Tapeworms aren't transmitted from dog to dog. Various tapeworms use deer, ground birds, rodents, or fleas as their secondary hosts. To become infected, the dog must eat part of one of these hosts. Fleas are probably the most common secondary host of tapeworms, and eating an infested flea can transmit the tapeworm to dogs.

This parasite differs from the others in that it usually can't be diagnosed by microscopic examination of a stool sample. The tapeworm head (scolex) remains attached to the lining of the dog's intestine. The tapeworm body is made up of segments and the worm grows to enormous lengths. As it grows, the segments break off and pass out in the stool. Diagnosis is made by finding small white segments of the tapeworm that look like tiny grains of rice stuck to the hair around Dandy's anus.

Tapeworms compete with their host for food. A heavily infested dog will appear unthrifty and thin, and often exhibit a dry coat.

Treatment is usually only half the problem, since controlling the dog's consumption of host material is as important as killing the parasite within the dog. This often means controlling the flea population, or preventing the dog from eating roadkill deer, rabbits, or other rodents.

Treating Worms

Worm medications are types of poisons. The average dog owner should leave the worm treatment to a trained veterinarian. If medication is dispensed by your veterinarian, be meticulous when calculating dosages and carefully administer the medication according to label directions.

An especially perilous procedure is to worm all puppies, whether or not a parasite infestation has been diagnosed. If Dandy isn't harboring parasites, don't treat him. *There is no excuse for doing something well that shouldn't be done at all.*

Heartworm

Mosquitoes transmit *Dirofilaria*, the larvae of heartworms. These micro-scopic immature worms develop in the mosquito for a couple of weeks, and are then injected into another dog by the mosquito. The larvae mature into adult heartworms, sometimes reaching 1 foot (30 cm) in length with the diameter of a matchstick. These adults live in the dog's heart. No immediate outward signs of disease are seen if only a few adult worms are present, but with a heavy infestation, the dog may suffer heart failure. An infected dog acts as a reservoir of infection for other dogs.

Formerly a threat only in high-moisture areas, in recent years, heartworm disease has spread to nearly every part of the United States, including Alaska. Before a preventive program can be initiated, a blood test must show that there are no larvae circulating in your dog's bloodstream. Heartworm prevention is accomplished by means of regular oral medication.

Heartworm life cycle can be interrupted with drugs.

Allergies

This condition is manifested in dozens of ways. Allergies can take the form of skin redness, stomach upsets, itching, or joint and muscle pain. It is possible for a dog to become allergic to practically anything. Commonly seen allergic reactions are associated with flea saliva, milk products, and irritating plants such as poison ivy or nettles. Dogs may become allergic to various medications, to endoparasites, and even to inhaled dusts or pollens.

In other words, allergies may be responsible for a multitude of vague signs in your dog. The diagnosis of allergies is sometimes easily made, while at other times it is nearly impossible. If Dandy displays strange signs of illness, note when they occur relative to walks, meals, sleep, and weather. Call your veterinarian, describe what you have observed, and seek professional advice. Some allergies are diagnosed by skin patch tests, others by trial and error food changes, and others by process of elimination.

Otitis Externa

Ear infections often are caused by foreign material in the ear canal or by bacteria that enter the canal and become established there. These infections are seen more often in floppy-eared dogs than in those with erect ears.

When wax builds up in the external ear canal, secondary infections may begin. Itch and irritation become unbearable, and the dog scratches violently causing serum to ooze into the canal and feeding the infecting bacteria. The ear canal must be thoroughly cleaned, and medication is applied into the canal. This usually means a trip to the veterinarian.

Grass Awns

Whether Dandy rarely leaves his big fenced yard or goes on frequent walks, he is likely to encounter cheat grass or wild oats. The awns or seedpods of those plants are attached to little beards that stick in your socks when you walk though the grass. Those same bearded awns can make their way into Dandy's ear canals, causing great discomfort and necessitating a trip to your veterinarian for removal.

If your dog is longhaired, his foot hair will pick up these grass awns. These nuisances must be removed promptly or the sharply pointed seeds may penetrate the skin and begin to migrate into the tissue, requiring minor surgery to remove them.

Ear Hematoma

Another condition seen most frequently in floppy-eared dogs is ear hematoma. This condition appears like a fat ear, and usually follows an ear infection. Regardless of the specific cause, the infected ear irritates the dog and causes him to shake his head violently. When he whips the ear, vessels are torn and a pocket of blood forms between layers of cartilage and skin.

This is another condition requiring professional help. First, the initial problem must be solved, then the pocket of blood serum is drained, usually by surgical means. The ear is immobilized for a time, and healing is usually uncomplicated.

Hereditary Conditions

Mixed breeds suffer from fewer hereditary conditions than do purebreds, but they aren't immune from them.

Eye Diseases

Eye conditions are often hereditary, but others are the natural result of aging. Some eye problems are related to the loose skin of the face, which occurs in mixed breeds and purebreds alike. Traumatic eye diseases are sometimes caused by inherited characteristics and are discussed in this section, though they may not always be related to genetics.

Progressive Retinal Atrophy: Progressive Retinal Atrophy (PRA) is a serious hereditary eye disease caused by degeneration of retinal cells, which leaves the dog unable to see stationary objects. It causes vision impairment by about five years of age.

Purebred breeding stock should be examined for this disease. Ask your veterinarian about the various certifying agencies such as CERF. Some affected dogs are treated, but cure is unlikely. A dog affected with PRA may lose his vision, but blindness isn't fatal. If the vision diminishes slowly, the dog will adapt and live a normal life span as a pet.

Entropion: A dog may inherit a predisposition for this condition, which may cause symptoms at any age. It is not a serious threat to the life or health of the dog, but if it is determined to be hereditary, affected dogs shouldn't be bred.

Entropion is caused by excess skin around the dog's eyes, which causes the lids of the eyes (upper or lower) to roll inward. With the rolling skin, the hair of the eyelids rubs on the dog's cornea, causing severe irritation. Secondary conjunctivitis usually accompanies entropion, and the dog often squints in discomfort.

This condition is easily repaired by a relatively simple surgical operation.

Ectropion: Ectropion is another surgically correctable eyelid problem. If too much loose facial skin causes the eyelids to droop excessively, the exposed conjunctiva is subject to infection. Predisposition for this condition is sometimes inherited, but may occur in mixed breeds.

Corneal Scratches and Ulcers: These are usually traumatic in nature, although in some breeds ulcers may occur spontaneously and are considered to be genetically transmitted. Simple dust irritation or foreign bodies such as grass seeds that are caught under the eyelids often cause dogs to scratch and rub at their eyes. Toenails can cause corneal scratches as well.

Immediate diagnosis and treatment is required. If neglected, the dog's constant rubbing may cause the cornea to rupture, and loss of vision results, sometimes accompanied by a loss of the eye.

Whenever Dandy squints, rubs his eye, holds it closed, and it appears reddened and inflamed, hasten him to your veterinarian!

Cherry Eye: The nictitating membrane, also called the third eyelid, usually appears as a tiny pink structure located at the inside corner (nasal canthus) of the eye. If that membrane becomes irritated, it expands over the entire eye surface. If the gland situated on the underneath side of the membrane becomes inflamed, it will swell and cause the entire third eyelid to turn inside out. This results in a horrible-appearing red mass, which, surprisingly, doesn't seem to bother the dog at all.

Cherry eye is easily diagnosed, and if no cause is found, can be treated either by surgical removal of the gland or sometimes by medication to combat the swelling and infection. A predisposition for cherry eye can be inherited.

Cataracts: Usually a condition seen in old dogs, cataracts may be hereditary. A cataract is an opacity within the lens, which lies immediately behind the iris. Eventually causing blindness, this condition can't be treated medically. Cataract or lens removal is surgically possible. Surgery is expensive, and even when done by specially trained veterinary ophthalmologists, it may have complications.

Glaucoma: This disease is often genetically transmitted. It results when the fluid pressure within the eyeball increases, causing significant discomfort and possibly blindness. Glaucoma is diagnosed with special veterinary equipment and is treated both medically and surgically with fair success.

Pigmentary Keratitis (PK): A condition caused by the invasion of blood vessels into the normally clear cornea, PK is usually genetically associated with certain breeds. German Shepherds are probably the breed in which this disease is seen most frequently. Invading vessels carry pigment into the cornea and deposit it there, and if allowed to progress unchecked, PK will eventually cause a physical obstruction to vision. The invasion of blood vessels can usually be controlled by the application of medication into the eye, or by injecting steroids into the juncture between the cornea and sclera (white) of the eye.

Limb Conditions

A few limb conditions exist that are commonly hereditary. Again, mixed breeds may suffer from these problems, but the percentage is greater in purebreds.

Canine Hip Dysplasia (CHD): This devastating problem always ranks number one when discussing hereditary limb disorders. It causes hind leg lameness that sometimes doesn't appear until the dog is an adult. CHD, or a predisposition to it, is undoubtedly hereditary, but in a complex way. It's prevalent to some degree in all large and in many small purebreds and is occasionally seen in mixed breeds as well. Dogs that have their hips x-rayed, have those X rays checked by the Orthopedic Foundation for Animals (OFA), and are certified clear of the disease, may still produce affected puppies. In fact, CHD may crop up in dogs from bloodlines that are certified *CHD-clear* for several generations. X rays taken before the dog is two years old are not conclusive.

CHD involves the head or ball of the femur and the acetabulum or

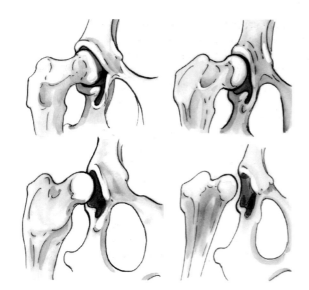

Hip dysplasia is manifested by deformities of joint and secondary arthritis.

pelvic hip socket. The acetabulum and femoral head are misshapen and don't fit together smoothly. In time, arthritis usually results from the condition, causing pain, inflammation, and lameness.

CHD is a relative condition; all dogs aren't equally affected. Lameness depends on the amount of displacement of the femoral head and the damage to the joint cartilage. Signs of CHD usually appear by two or three years of age, but occasionally they are delayed as late as six or seven. Signs of CHD may appear in one hind leg (unilateral) or both hind legs (bilateral) causing pain, difficulty in getting up from a lying or sitting position, and lameness when walking. It may progress to a level where the dog can't get up or walk. Those

dogs are usually thin, and in pain most of the time.

Treatments include hip replacement and other surgical techniques to relieve pain, acupuncture, anti-inflammatory drugs, and more recently, polysulfated glycosaminoglycan (PSGAG), with or without chondroitin. This product seems to stimulate the repair of cartilage and shows promise. No treatment or medication will cure the disease, and only the prudent selection of breeding stock can prevent the condition from occurring.

Elbow Dysplasia: Another hereditary condition, un-united anconeal process, or elbow dysplasia is a developmental disease causing great pain and debility. It is prevalent in a few breeds; it may appear in many. Treatable by surgical intervention or conservatively with medication, it remains a serious disease.

Luxated Patella: This stifle (knee) disease is more common in toy purebreds, although it is a problem in many breeds and is seen occasionally in mixed breeds. When the knee is flexed, the patella or kneecap slides up and down in a groove in the lower end of the femur or thighbone. Sometimes this groove is too shallow or the patella is malformed. The ligaments holding the kneecap in place may be weak, or the lower leg bone doesn't hinge well with the femur due to poor angulation. In any case, the patella slips out of its appointed position (becomes luxated), and the dog limps or carries the leg.

The diagnosis is simple and can be proven by X ray; treatment may be effected by various surgical procedures.

Other Genetic Diseases

Several other conditions are common to all purebred dogs and some mixed breeds.

Monorchidism: Male dogs are born with both testicles positioned in their abdomens. Soon after birth, or in 30 or 40 days, the testicles should be descended into a male puppy's scrotum. Monorchidism occurs when one testicle is retained in the dog's abdomen. This testicular retention is hereditary, but the exact genetic mechanism is poorly understood.

Monorchid males are able to breed and are fertile but such dogs should be castrated at or soon after puberty because retained testicles often develop malignant tumors. Due to the hereditability of monorchidism, males with a retained testicle should never be used in a breeding program.

Cryptorchidism: Cryptorchids are males with both testicles retained in the abdomen. They will mount and breed females, but usually are unable to produce offspring. Cryptorchid dogs should be castrated at or shortly after reaching puberty to prevent development of malignant tumors later in life.

Epilepsy: A seizure disorder said to be inherited in many cases, epilepsy may also result from injury, tumors, or possibly infections. Unfortunately, when it is hereditary, the seizures don't begin until the affected dog is several years old, and it is thus difficult to breed out of a strain or bloodline.

Epileptic seizures are often brief, and the dog returns to normal within a few minutes. Veterinarians usually diagnose the condition by owners' reports, but in some cases, the seizure lasts long enough for the dog to make the trip to a veterinarian. The condition is usually treatable with daily or twice daily medication. No cure is known. Untreated, the seizures may become more frequent and more severe and eventually cause death.

Miscellaneous Intestinal Diseases

The following discussion describes some common canine intestinal problems seen occasionally in all dogs.

A Border Collie glides over the jump.

Gastric Torsion, Dilatation, and Bloat

This condition is commonly seen in large and giant breeds and sometimes in big crossbred dogs. There are many theories as to the cause of this often-fatal condition.

Allowing your big dog to exercise following a heavy meal is a factor that promotes gastric torsion. Another is the practice of feeding the large dog on the floor or ground.

About two to six hours after a meal, an affected dog's stomach distends with gas and twists on its long axis. This twisting prevents the gas from escaping by belching. The patient repeatedly attempts to vomit, but is unable to do so and spits thick saliva in small amounts. A veterinarian may attempt to pass a stomach tube to relieve the stomach gas, but due to the twist, those efforts are often futile.

Bloat causes intense abdominal pain, which is accompanied by shock. Immediate surgery may save the pet, but unfortunately by the time the dog reaches a veterinary hospital, he may be suffering from advanced toxemia and efforts to save the patient may be too late.

There are a number of measures you can take that will help prevent this condition from developing in Dandy. Feed him when his physical activity is minimal. Elevate his food bowl by setting it on a porch step, which will minimize swallowing air. Feed frequent, small meals or give him free-choice feeding. If you find it necessary to feed a large meal, make sure he remains quiet for an hour thereafter. Don't allow him to engorge with water following a meal. Above all, curtail Dandy's activity after any meal.

Esophagitis, Enteritis, Gastritis, and Colitis

The esophagus, stomach, small intestine, large intestine, and rectum are confluent and together are known as the gastrointestinal tract or simply the gut. The suffix -itis means inflammation of; thus, esophagitis is an inflammation of the esophagus, gastritis is an inflammation of the stomach, enteritis is an inflammation of the small intestine, and colitis is an inflammation of the large intestine or the lower bowel. These gut irritations are commonly accompanied by diarrhea or vomiting. In most cases, gastritis is accompanied by a degree of enteritis, and enteritis usually has some colitis associated with it. In other words, the single word diagnoses are rarely technically correct.

When your veterinarian tells you that Dandy is suffering from gastroenteritis, the cause of the gut irritation is more important than the diagnostic term applied. If Dandy exhibits watery diarrhea, vomiting, nausea, depression, and lack of normal appetite, we might think of food or chemical poisoning, but gastroenteritis might be caused by eating indigestible material such as a steel wool pot scrubber. The same signs can be an indication of liver cancer. It is important to remember that a gut irritation is a signal that might mean a serious, even life-threatening, condition, and should never be taken lightly.

Constipation

Another type of gut problem is blockage or impaction. Most commonly seen in older dogs, constipation is often caused by bone chips and pieces. Dandy finds a nice juicy bone. He virtually consumes the tasty morsel over the next hour, and swallows every bite. Bone pieces are not very digestible, so, when these little chips reach the rectum where fluid is extracted from the waste, the result is a concrete block in the lower bowel. The same result may be seen when a dog licks and swallows masses of its hair.

As a blockage forms, Dandy's gut fills with food and waste that can't escape, and he loses his appetite and becomes lethargic. Diagnosis is usually made by a veterinarian's palpation of the solid mass in Dandy's lower bowel. Treatment is usually done by enemas, which will supply liquids to the mass, break it up, and enable the dog to pass the impaction.

Pseudocoprostasis or False Constipation

This condition is common to longhaired dogs of all ages, and usually is the result of soft stools and grooming neglect. It occurs when the long hair in the vicinity of the anus is not routinely trimmed or combed and becomes matted with feces. The fecal mat acts as a blockage of the gut, and signs similar to true constipation are seen.

Diagnosis is simple and can usually be made from across the room by the smell. Treatment is even simpler, though not very pleasant to perform. The long hair and fecal mats must be carefully cut away to expose the skin surrounding the anal opening.

Old Dog Diseases

Among these conditions are several diseases of unspayed bitches. Menopause does not occur in female canines. By about six years of age, a bitch has passed her productive peak, although she continues to cycle and exhibit normal heat periods. Reproductive problems and the bitch's health risks are likely to increase with each passing year. *Ovariohysterectomy is the best insurance policy you can buy for your female dog.*

Metritis and Pyometra (Uterine Infection)

These two uterine diseases affect unspayed bitches. Metritis is sometimes fatal in young and middle-aged females, but its danger is multiplied many times in older animals. It can be averted by ovariohysterectomy.

Pyometra is an extremely dangerous type of metritis and occurs most commonly in older, unspayed females.

Mammary Tumors

Breast tumors account for nearly half of all canine tumor cases, and at least half of all breast tumors are malignant. They may occur at any age, but are more common in females past six years old. If spayed at or before puberty, the risk of mammary tumors is negligible, but each time the bitch comes in heat, her predisposition for these tumors increases.

Arthritis

Just as you and I can look forward to some joint pain later in life, Dandy may have similar experiences. Hip joints are most commonly affected, but with age, virtually every joint is subject to the pain of arthritis.

Your veterinarian can best advise you about the proper treatment for arthritis. Nonsteroidal anti-inflamma-tory drugs such as ibuprofen, buffered aspirin, and some of the drugs and treatments mentioned in the hip dysplasia discussion (page 107) may be of value. Acetaminophen may be used to dispel pain. Old dogs' digestive tracts are somewhat sensitive, and *no drug should be used without calling your veterinarian*.

Skin Cysts and Tumors

As dogs age, small wartlike tumors may spring up like mush-rooms after a rain. These little skin tumors are frequently seen on the old dog's face and legs. Other, larger growths that are often diag-nosed as lipomas or fatty tumors tend to show up on the abdomen or back. Cysts, or hollow growths filled with sticky thick fluid, are also found on many older dogs.

Your veterinarian often diagnoses these benign masses when Dandy is presented for his annual old dog checkup. Treatment depends on the age and general health of the individual and the size and position of the masses. If Dandy is quite old, and the masses aren't causing him any discomfort, they are usually ignored. Unfortunately, none of us will look as beautiful in our golden years as when we are young.

Calluses

Calluses are benign thickenings of skin over pressure points. Most commonly seen on elbows, they may appear on the lower legs and hips as well. They have no significance unless they become irritated or infected. Calluses result from lying on concrete or other hard surfaces; they may be minimized by providing Dandy with a blanket or foam pad placed in his favorite napping place.

Deafness

Deafness is another aging condition. Sometimes it's difficult to judge whether a wise old dog is actually losing his hearing or is selectively deciding what sounds he will respond to. If Dandy is losing his hearing, its best to stamp your foot when you approach him, so he will not be surprised by your touch. Hearing aids have not yet been marketed for dogs, so deafness must be gracefully accepted and generally ignored.

Dental Disease

If you have taken care of Dandy's teeth in his youth, they will probably reflect this care when he is old. In case you have forgotten to brush daily, and if he isn't provided with chew bones, he may suffer from dental problems later in life. Usually, loose and infected teeth will be discovered on annual checkups, but if Dandy seems sensitive when he eats, look for dental problems.

Diagnosis is made by a foul odor emanating from his mouth, tenderness when he chews, picking up and immediately spitting out his food, and lack of interest in chew sticks.

Your veterinarian can clean or extract teeth as needed. Sometimes, an anesthetic will be required for this service, and the risk-benefit aspect of dental treatment should always be discussed with the doctor.

Obesity

Though not usually thought of as a disease, obesity is a serious threat to older dogs. Obesity may be an early warning of several metabolic diseases such as diabetes, hypothyroidism, Cushing's disease, and others. Even when not associated with an underlying disease, obesity will shorten the life of your dog by stressing leg joints and internal organ function, and should never be ignored. Schedule an appointment with your veterinarian for a laboratory workup to rule out systemic diseases. If Dandy is simply overweight, begin a careful reducing plan, one that won't cause undue stress.

If weight loss is your goal:
• Reduce Dandy's total food intake and feed him several small meals

daily instead of one or two larger meals.

• Add cooked carrots as a filler to satisfy his appetite.

• Use low-calorie dog foods that contain a complete nutritional balance, vitamins, and minerals.

• Don't subscribe to crash diets; with your veterinarian's advice, plan to reduce Dandy's weight over a period of months.

• Carefully begin an exercise program. Take him for short walks daily, or if possible several times daily. To increase his desire to exercise, take him to new places where he can pick up new smells and sights.

• Months or sometimes years may be added to an obese dog's life by weight reduction and appropriate exercise.

Diabetes Mellitus

Diabetes is a metabolic disease most often seen in older dogs. It is manifested by lethargy, excessive water consumption, increased urination, and weight gain. Later in the course of the disease, sudden weight loss and vomiting are exhibited. If you suspect diabetes in your dog, take him to the veterinarian for laboratory work. This disease is treatable, but success depends on early diagnosis.

Euthanasia

This is a subject saved for last because we hate to discuss it. How do you know when the time has come to give Dandy up? It would be convenient if he just passed away in his sleep, but, unfortunately, it rarely happens that way. Old dogs often become infirm, suffering from constant pain. Their eyes will plead with you to do something to help them, but there is nothing more you can do.

Euthanasia is the final act of love, kindness, and stewardship we can perform for our loyal canine companions. When a trusted veterinarian administers the lethal injection, the dog suffers no fear or apprehension. If you find it in your heart to stay with your old friend, do so; he will appreciate it. Being there will let him know you haven't abandoned him, and your presence will reassure him.

Why and How

There are many reasons for giving your old friend a painless departure from this world; all are associated with a single factor: Life has become a painful, confusing burden to the old dog. Perhaps Dandy's senses have failed and he no longer has any pleasure or comfort in life. Maybe his arthritis or chronic disease has progressed painfully beyond help, and every day is torture for him. Perhaps organ failure has defeated his will to live. Generally, your canine companion will tell you when it is time.

Administration of a lethal injection should always be done without anxiety on the part of the dog, the veterinarian, the assistant, and the owner. The veterinarian should handle Dandy gently and calmly, speaking to him in comforting tones. The injection should be prepared in advance, so the dog won't be alarmed by the syringe being filled in his presence. An assistant should steady the dog. Your veterinarian should make the venipuncture quickly, aspirate to insure the needle is seated in the vein, and rapidly inject the lethal fluid. Death will come instantly and without discomfort.

Why Not To

There are hundreds of bad reasons why a dog is put to sleep. Veterinarians have heard them all.

Dogs require training, a human responsibility. If you haven't taken the time to train Dandy, and teach him good manners, that's not a fair reason for euthanasia.

If you suddenly find his feeding and care are more trouble than he is worth, that's also a human problem, not an excuse for ending his life.

He's old, but age alone is no reason to give him up.

He's ill or has been injured; surgery, medication, and aftercare are more of an expense than you can afford. Have you explored every avenue available to you for financial help? Rescue organizations, no-kill animal aid institutions, and others may provide veterinary care.

You are moving away. This is a common excuse for giving up a valuable companion. Today, rescue associations and foster homes save many of these pets. Contact your local pound, shelter, or breed club for advice. Veterinarians often can put you in touch with no-kill facilities. Give Dandy another chance!

When Your Dog Dies

When you are ready for another dog, don't search for Dandy's clone. Dogs are individuals with different personalities; there isn't another dog *just like Dandy*. If he was a purebred, similar-appearing and similar-acting dogs may be found. Maybe another pup from the same kennel will be closely related to him, but it will never *take Dandy's place*.

Often it's best to seek another dog that is quite different in appearance, a different sex, another size. If Dandy was a purebred, try another breed. If he was of mixed heritage, try a dissimilar puppy. Don't put undue pressure on a new dog. Don't expect him to live up to his predecessor in personality, looks, performance, or trainability. It's unrealistic to expect him to copy the actions and thoughts of another dog he has never met.

Support Groups

Most small animal veterinarians can provide information about support groups to help you through the loss of your canine companion. Many of these same veterinarians have brochures that will give you information and support. Regardless of the reason for Dandy's death, you will grieve your loss; you will miss him more than you think. Comfort yourself by attending group support meetings; if none are available, start a group. It's natural to grieve the passing of a good friend, and it's easier to bear when discussed with others.

Chapter Nine

Brief Descriptions of Popular Breeds

Sporting Group

Labrador Retriever

Origin: Labradors usually are thought to have their origin in New-foundland, very likely from ancestors in the Saint John variety of the New-foundland breed. According to most accounts, they were introduced into England in the 1830s, and are known to have come to America early in the twentieth century. Their progenitors probably included Flat-coated Retrievers, Curly-coated Retrievers, and the smaller of the two varieties of Newfoundland. However, there is evidence that fish-ermen of Devon, England, actually bred them, later transported them to Newfoundland, and still later re-introduced these fine water dogs to Great Britain.

Aptitude: Labradors were origi-nally used to help Newfoundland fishermen haul in their loaded nets. More recently this intelligent breed has found numerous other uses.

The Lab is a fine companion ani-mal, and properly trained can be a valuable all-around gundog. A strong swimmer and natural retriever of aquatic and upland game birds, it requires very little special training.

Labradors are often candidates for guide dog training. Their fantastic innate scenting ability makes them quite useful as search-and-rescue, contraband, explosive, and drug-sniffing dogs.

Size: Males weigh 60 to 75 pounds (27 to 34 kg) and stand 22.5 to 24.5 inches (56 to 61 cm) tall. Females weigh 55 to 79 pounds (25 to 35 kg) and stand 21.5 to 23.5 inches (47 to 51 cm) tall.

Coat: A Labrador's coat is short and quite thick, with no waves or curls. It has a weather-resistant, tight undercoat. The Lab's coat is not feathered, and should be hard to the touch.

Colors: This breed is seen in three colors, black, chocolate, or yellow. Yellow Labs vary from fox-red to light cream-colored. Choco-late colors range from light sedge to dark chocolate. A small white spot on the chest is permissible in any color, but white appearing elsewhere is prohibited. Eye colors vary from black, brown, or hazel to yellow.

The nose-rubber should be black or dark brown, and a pink color is penalized in shows.

Coat care and exercise: The short coat of a Labrador is easily cared for. Daily or at least weekly brushing is best, with more intense combing and brushing during seasonal shedding.

Being an active sporting dog, the Lab's exercise requirements should not be overlooked. These are large, active dogs that thrive on regular, vigorous exercise. If they don't receive routine exercise, Labradors will invariably become obese.

Attitude: The average Labrador is a tough, gentle, and loyal companion dog that is patient and good-natured with children. Dogs of this breed are not known for their guard dog propensities, but they often become quite protective toward their owners' families and property. The Labrador is usually considered very intelligent and trainable, and gets along well with other pets. It is obedient, trustworthy, affectionate, and sociable. Although mentally and physically it matures later in life than some breeds, it has great strength and is a hard-working field dog.

Training: As in all large breeds, the Lab should receive the usual house-training and obedience training early in life.

Cocker Spaniel

Origin: The American Cocker evolved from the English Cocker,

Labrador Retriever.

which it closely resembles. It is a bit smaller than its English counterpart, usually has more coat, and has a different body conformation. This small English breed has a common origin with the English Toy Spaniel, Springer, English Cocker Spaniel, and other similar dogs of Great Britain. It probably originated from the careful crossing of setters with smaller spaniels. In the seventeenth century these breeds were divided into water and land spaniels, and further divided into small and large spaniels. From the smaller land spaniels came the ancestors of the American Cocker. The name "cocker" is derived from "cocking spaniel," or one used to flush and retrieve woodcocks. The American version of Cockers is generally considered the smallest sporting dog breed.

Aptitude: The Cocker Spaniel is quiet, keen, and industrious, of particular value as a companion dog. It is an intelligent, energetic, and playful dog, having a gentle disposition with children. Said to possess the sweetest temperament of the sporting dogs, the Cocker isn't known for timidity, but should be handled gently. As with most other small dogs, yelling and threatening can easily upset the Cocker.

Field trials for Cockers were begun in the United States in 1924. Retaining much of their innate hunting instinct, few Cockers are used as field dogs today. With training and encouragement, the Cocker will flush and retrieve upland game birds for the patient hunter. When so used, the Cocker is trained to quarter close to the gunner, and drop or sit when birds are flushed.

Cocker Spaniel.

Size: Males weigh about 28 pounds (13 kg) and stand approximately 15 inches (38 cm) tall. Females are slightly smaller, weighing about 26 pounds (11 kg) and standing approximately 14 inches (35 cm) tall.

Coat: Ears, chest, abdomen, and legs are well feathered with long, silky, flat, or slightly wavy hair that is relatively easily maintained. On the head, the hair is short and fine; on the body it is medium length. It is silky, flat, or slightly wavy.

Colors: Cockers are shown separately as black, ASCOB (any solid color other than black), which includes the various shades of tan and red, and parti-color, which includes two or more definite well-broken colors, one of which must be white.

Coat care and exercise: Grooming is very important in this breed. Thorough brushing and combing an adult should be done every day, or no less than three times weekly, and Cockers should be trimmed and professionally groomed every four weeks. This is a limiting factor to ownership; if you haven't time for grooming, you probably shouldn't acquire this breed.

Attitude: The Cocker is sociable and easily accepts people, other dogs, and most other house pets. It usually has a sweet temperament, and is keen and industrious. It is a merry, peaceable, playful, and intelligent pet with an effervescent disposition. Although originally bred as a gundog, it is generally now thought of as a companion.

Training: These gentle dogs should be trained with an eye to their amiable dispositions. Cockers are sensitive, but alert and easily trained. They will usually respond to the tone of your voice, and shouldn't be intimidated or nagged.

Golden Retriever

Origin: An often-repeated story relates that Goldens were first bred in Brighton, England, by Sir Dudley Majoribanks from a troupe of eight Russian circus dogs. These performing dogs traced their ancestry to Russian Trackers. Sir Dudley crossed the original Goldens with Bloodhounds to reduce their giant size.

A more likely history begins with Lord Tweedmouth of Invernessshire, Scotland, and tells of breeding Goldens from Tweed Water Spaniels, Newfoundlands, Irish Setters, and possibly Flat-coated Retrievers. Originally called Yellow Retrievers, Goldens were first shown in England in 1908, and were listed as Flat Coats (Golden). In 1911 they were recognized as a separate breed and the Golden Retriever Club of England was formed.

Aptitude: This breed was originally bred as a gundog and retriever. Its primary aptitude still lies in sporting events where it excels in retriever trials. Today, it is well suited to all kinds of fieldwork, as well as obedience trials. It is a valuable all-around gundog, companion, therapy dog, and assistance dog, and is in demand as a guide dog for the blind. Goldens are among the best family pets.

Golden Retriever.

Size: Males weigh 65 to 75 pounds and stand 23 to 24 inches (56 to 61 cm) tall. Females weigh 55 to 65 pounds (25 to 29 kg) and stand 21 to 22.5 inches (51 to 56 cm) tall.

Coat: Golden coats are dense, water-repellent, soft, wavy, and smooth. Feathering is seen on the back of the forelegs and the underbody, with heavier feathering on the front of the neck and underside of the tail.

Colors: Lustrous colors of cream and various shades of golden are allowed. Small groups of white hairs on the chest are sometimes seen.

Coat care and exercise: The golden coat is easily cared for with weekly brushing and bathing when needed.

Being a large, outdoor, sporting dog, it requires regular exercise, although it is quick to adapt to a family's lifestyle. It delights in swimming and walks when not being used in the field.

Attitude: A Golden's impeccable character is its most delightful characteristic. Even-tempered and gentle, this dog is also a strong, tough gundog. Its intelligence is well documented, and it is among the most affectionate and obedient companions. Eager to please, this dog's even, predictable temperament makes it an invaluable family pet. It is quite trainable, and one of the most desirable weekend gundogs. It adapts well to other pets, and is a wonderful children's playmate.

Training: Puppy training can begin as early as eight weeks, and should be continued throughout the dog's life. Easily trained, the Golden thrives on new challenges. It possesses a reliable memory, and rarely forgets anything it has learned.

Many Golden Retrievers hold advanced titles in obedience work, and they also excel in tracking.

English Springer Spaniel

Origin: One of the largest spaniels, the English Springer is closely related to the English Cocker, both originating in England in spite of its Spanish-derived name. The Springer is a land spaniel and originally was used to *spring* or flush game for Greyhounds or falcons.

Aptitude: Like other spaniels, the English Springer's greatest joy is in the field. It is truly a dual-purpose dog, finding use both as a hunting dog and a family pet. It is a gentle, friendly companion and an energetic, biddable hunter. Playful, loyal, and intelligent, the Springer is also an excellent natural guard dog.

Size: Males weigh 49 to 55 pounds (22 to 25 kg) and stand 20 inches (51 cm) tall. Females weigh about 49 pounds (22 kg) and stand 19 inches (48 cm) tall.

Coat: Springer coats are dense, smooth, and well feathered, with short, fine hair being found on the head and front of forelegs. The coat is flat or wavy, and waterproof.

Colors: Black or liver and white; black or liver and white with tan accent markings; blue; blue roan are all permissible. All degrees of ticking are seen with these colors. Lemon, red, or orange is penalized.

Coat care and exercise: The fine coat of a Springer requires regular brushing, and most also need professional trimming several times a

English Springer Spaniel.

year. This dog's long ears and foot hair require regular care as well.

The Springer is an active dog requiring regular, vigorous exercise. Swimming is an excellent exercise for it when possible, and regular runs in the country or park will help. Exercise is a major consideration when choosing a Springer as a family pet.

Attitude: The personality of a Springer is generally well suited to active families and individuals who can spend lots of time playing and exercising their dogs. It is a friendly, sociable dog that displays unusual cunning and intelligence. Obedient and eager to please, these dogs are excellent pets.

Training: *Early* training is important in this strong breed. Handling, bonding, and obedience training will enhance the value of the Springer as a companion pet. When approached in a logical, stepwise fashion, training should be trouble-free.

German Shorthaired Pointer

Origin: This breed originated in Germany and was bred from Spanish Pointers, English Foxhounds, and Bloodhounds. A fairly recent addition to American hunting, the first ones were imported to the United States in about 1920.

Aptitude: A hunting dog through and through, this versatile dog has been successfully used to hunt pheasant, quail, grouse, partridge, snipe, woodcock, ducks, rabbits, coon, possum, and occasionally deer. German Shorthairs have excel-

German Shorthaired Pointer.

lent noses, and are biddable and talented pointers that combine good bird sense with retrieving ability.

Size: Males weigh 55 to 70 pounds (25 to 32 kg) and stand 23 to 25 inches (63 to 65 cm) tall. Females weigh 45 to 60 pounds (20 to 27 kg) and stand 21 to 23 inches (53 to 57 cm) tall.

Coat: The Shorthair coat is tight and lies close to the body. The hair is short, thick, and tough.

Colors: Liver or any combination of liver and white, including spotting, ticking, or liver roan are allowed. Dogs with black, red, orange, lemon, or tan markings, and all-white dogs are disqualified.

Coat care and exercise: The Shorthair coat is trouble-free and easy to care for. Brushing with a slicker brush, chamois, or rubber currycomb is all it needs.

Typical of sporting breeds, the Shorthair thrives on exercise. This dog is best placed in a sportive family who get to the field regularly. It likes to be kept busy and won't fit well in sedentary surroundings. If you are thinking of owning a Shorthair, but live in an apartment, think again.

Attitude: Primarily, this is a hunting breed, one of the foremost upland bird pointers and retrievers of the nation. In this regard, it is an excellent pet for weekend hunters who also have large yards.

As a companion dog, the Shorthair is active and intelligent. It requires interaction with its family and is perfectly at home in a household environment, if exercise and diversion are provided. Although usually friendly, with strangers it may be reserved and vigilant, and some references include *short-tempered* in this breed's description.

Brittany.

Training: Training should start early rather than later. When properly trained, this dog is eager to please, biddable, and willing to learn. Consistency is the key to good training.

Brittany

Origin: Named for the French province of Brittany, this old breed was originally named Brittany Spaniel. It is said to be the progeny of several European breeds including the Red and White Setter and the French Braque de Bourbonnais Pointer. It came to America in about 1931 after becoming a favorite in its native land.

Aptitude: The Brittany is truly a dual-purpose dog. Its popularity with hunters and field trial enthusiasts is about as strong as with dog show devotees. As a gundog it has an exceptional nose and will retrieve waterfowl with nearly the same talent as it does upland birds.

This breed is often found in backyards, and is quite popular as a family dog.

Size: Males weigh 30 to 40 pounds (13.5 to 18 kg) and stand 17.5 to 20.5 inches (44 to 51 cm) tall. Females are only slightly smaller with no specific size difference given in the standard.

Coat: The Brittany's coat is flat, dense, and wavy with a medium texture and not much feathering. Neither silky nor curly, the coat is easily cared for.

Colors: Orange and white or liver and white colors predominate, but roan patterns and ticking are desirable. Black is a disqualification.

Coat care and exercise: The Brittany is among the easiest breeds to groom. Regular combing and brushing should take no more than a few minutes several times weekly. Exercise is another matter. The active Brittany, like other active bird dogs, requires regular, extensive exercise. Bored, inactive dogs often develop nuisance habits.

Attitude: The sweet-tempered Brit is an ideal dog to own. It is a playful, gentle, and loyal companion, a determined and dedicated hunter. This dog fits well into active families who hunt on weekends. It is a curious, obedient dog that thrives on attention and training.

Training: Intelligence is a long suit of the Brittany. This highly trainable dog loves interaction with its owner, and in some circles is known as a one-man dog. Obedience training and tracking provide other interests for this breed.

Weimaraner

Origin: Originally called the Weimar Pointer, this breed began in Germany as a gundog. It is said to be kin to both the German Shorthaired Pointer and the Bloodhound.

Aptitude: The Gray Ghost is a strong-willed but obedient hunting dog that points and retrieves well in the field and is most appreciated by those who hunt several times weekly. It is a rough and rowdy dog with great stamina that is best suited to hunting and outdoor families.

Weimaraner.

Size: Males weigh 57 to 77 pounds (30 to 37 kg) and stand 25 to 27 inches (62 to 67 cm) tall. Females weigh 55 to 70 pounds (22 to 31 kg) and stand 23 to 25 inches (57 to 62 cm) tall.

Coat: In its country of origin, it is still known in two coat types, long-haired and shorthaired, but the American Registry recognizes only the shorthaired variety. Its hair is quite sleek and lays tight.

Colors: Mouse gray to silver gray are the only colors recognized. There may be slight blending of color to lighter shades on the head.

Coat care and exercise: This dog's slick coat requires very little care; occasional brushing with a chamois or rubber currycomb will keep the coat in shape. Exercise is another matter as the Weimaraner is not a city dog, and has a need for extensive work and exercise.

Attitude: Often too much for small children to handle, this dog is better suited to adult families. It is protective yet friendly to those whom it knows.

Training: Like most hunting dogs, the Weimaraner delights in field training and prefers to be hunting or training. It is a dominant breed that requires a strong trainer and regular work.

Hound Group

Dachshund

Origin: This short-legged, long, little dog hails from Germany where it was bred to burrow into badger dens and haul out prey.

Aptitude: Originally a hunting dog, the Dachshund has evolved as a tough, strong, little companion dog.

Wirehaired Dachshund.

It is equipped with more courage than most small dogs, and makes an excellent family dog. Tough and hardy, the Doxie is a resilient pet.

Size: This breed is shown in two sizes, standard and miniature, and in three coat types, smooth, long-haired, and wirehaired. The standards weigh more than 11 pounds (5 kg), usually between 16 and 32 pounds (7.3 to 14.6 kg) and stand about 8 to 9 inches (20 to 25 cm) tall. Miniatures weigh less than 11 pounds (5 kg) and stand 5 to 6 inches (12.5 to 15 cm) tall.

Coat: Coats vary from short and smooth to long and wavy to rough and wiry. Each has its particular quality described in the breed standard.

Colors: Dachshunds are seen in all shades of red or brown with the possibility of dapples, double dapples, and shadings of sable or cream and black.

Coat care and exercise: Although varying according to coat type, the dachshund is easily groomed. The longhaired variety requires daily brushing, but little or no trimming. Occasional brushing and combing is sufficient maintenance for the wirehaired and smooth varieties.

Attitude: The Dachshund is a brave, rather dominant dog. It is known to be resourceful and curious, and is a tenacious guard dog. Quite protective of its children, it is loyal to its family and often shuns the acquaintance of strangers. The hunting instinct remains in this breed, and digging and burrowing is a favorite pastime.

Training: Patience is required to own a Dachshund. Due to its strong will, it requires constant training tune-ups. It is said to be obedient, if not slavish, in its response to commands.

Beagle

Origin: This trailing hound originates from Great Britain. Used for hunting rabbits or hares, this is the smallest of the trailing hounds.

Aptitude: This little hound has a terrific nose, and when lost, it can usually be found following a trail of some kind. It is usually a fine family pet due to its size, coat type, and hardiness. It accommodates well to children and other pets, and when used for hunting rabbits or squirrels, it is ecstatic.

Size: Shown in two separate varieties: the 13-inch (33-cm), which are less than 13 inches tall, and the 15-inch (38-cm), which are 13 to 15 inches tall. Beagles weigh between 18 and 30 pounds (8 to 14 kg). Note: The Pocket Beagle was a popular size at one time, standing less than 10 inches (25 cm).

Coat: Beagles have close, medium-length hair that is dense and hard-textured.

Colors: Any true hound color is permissible, including almost any combination of tan, black, and white, and clearly defined markings.

Coat care and exercise: The close coat of a Beagle requires no more than brushing every few days with a rubber currycomb or stiff bristle brush.

Beagles.

Attitude: The Beagle has a sweet temperament that is well adapted to family life, but it makes a rather poor watchdog. It is a wonderful playmate for children, and since its heritage is pack-oriented, it behaves well around other pets when introduced as youths. When bored, it is swift to find diversion, which often leads it to wander. Equipped with a fine hound *bay*, it can be heard for miles when on a trail.

Training: The Beagle isn't known to be extremely obedient and is sometimes slow to respond. It is a resolute and vigilant little hound that has a mind of its own. Training must be initiated early, be consistent, and be regularly practiced. Obedience classes are recommended for pet Beagles.

Basset Hound

Origin: *Basset* is derived from the French word meaning low or dwarf. Most Basset breeds originated in France and were bred from Bloodhounds. The Basset Hound that we know came to the United States

Basset Hound.

Coat care and exercise: Regular cleaning with a rubber grooming mitt is usually all the care this coat requires. Exercise the Basset moderately but regularly. Although playful, these hounds require less exercise than most hounds.

Attitude: The Basset, like most hounds, has a mind of its own. It is a loveable, sociable dog with a sense of humor. It hates to be left alone, and a pair is often easier to keep than a single one. Trustworthy with most other dogs, it should be introduced carefully to household pets when puppies. Because of its rather sedentary lifestyle, overeating and obesity are often seen in this breed.

Training: Patience and consistency in training is required. The Basset has a mind of its own. That characteristic and its rather gnarled legs and usual lackadaisical attitude make it a bit difficult to train in obedience work.

Norwegian Elkhound

Origin: Originating in Norway, with Vikings as its early owners, this breed is quite old. Skeletons of Stone Age Elkhoundlike dogs have been found in Scandinavia. For centuries this Spitzlike dog has been bred as a guard dog with herding instincts, and was used also to trail and tackle elk.

Aptitude: A natural hunting dog, the Elkhound has an excellent nose and enough toughness to handle big game. It has a gentle nature, hardiness, and other traits that make it an excellent family dog.

from England, probably with its roots in France.

Aptitude: The Basset Hound has the nose, ears, and voice of much bigger trail hounds. It is a superb children's companion, and gets along well with other pets. Its deep hound-dog voice is an early warning device that may frighten away strangers. Bred as trail hounds, Bassets have retained many of their hunting instincts.

Size: Bassets weigh 40 to 60 pounds (18 to 27 kg) and stand no more than 14 inches (35 cm) tall. Females are usually slightly smaller than males.

Coat: The Basset Hound has a hard, smooth, short coat that is dense and weather-resistant.

Colors: Any true hound colors are acceptable: black, white and tan, or brown. Distribution of colors and markings are not important.

Size: Males weigh 55 pounds (25 kg) and stand 20.5 inches (51 cm) tall. Females weigh 48 pounds (23 kg) and stand 19.5 inches (43 cm) tall.

Coat: This northern dog has a dense, wooly undercoat with thick, hard guard hair. It is a weatherproof insulation and lays smooth.

Colors: The preferred color is medium gray, but variations are seen due to the variations in the quantity of black-tipped guard hair. The undercoat is silver; the coat is the darkest on the saddle.

Coat care and exercise: This thick coat requires little grooming except during seasonal shedding. Like other northern breeds, it is dirt- and water-resistant. This active dog requires daily exercise, and should be in homes that match that need.

Attitude: The Elkhound is friendly and gentle and somewhat reserved with strangers. It is affectionate, although dominant at times. It is better suited for older children who understand the dog's temperament. It is not a great guard dog, although it will usually sound an alarm when strangers approach.

Training: Being an independent dog, the Norwegian Elkhound needs training, and responds well to firmness and affection without abuse or scolding. Consistency is a special trait of good Elkhound trainers.

Rhodesian Ridgeback

Origin: This interesting dog hails from Zimbabwe, South Africa, where it was bred by the Boer farmers as a

Norwegian Elkhound.

lion-hunting dog. The characteristic ridge that runs down the dog's back relates to its crossing with a half-wild dog of the Hottentots. The Ridgeback has been used to flush partridge, water buffaloes, and prowlers.

Aptitude: Outstanding as a guard dog and family protector, the Ridgeback is an excellent hunting dog with both sight- and scent-trailing attributes, great strength, and stamina. It is never quarrelsome with other dogs, and obedient to its master.

Size: Males weigh 75 pounds (30 kg) and stand 25 to 27 inches (63 to 68 cm) tall. Females weigh 65 pounds (30 kg) and stand 23 to 25 inches (60 to 66 cm) tall.

Coat: The Rhodesian Ridgeback's coat is dense, sleek, and

Rhodesian Ridgeback.

glossy. It has a strip of hair that grows contrary to the rest of the coat, and extends down the spine.

Colors: The characteristic color is a rich, reddish wheaten; the dog has a black mask.

Coat care and exercise: It is easy to maintain the coat; rubber currycomb brushing to remove the dead hairs is required. This is a hunting dog, and should be exercised accordingly. It becomes moody and melancholy if it does not get ample exercise.

Attitude: Fantastic stamina is this dog's hallmark. The Ridgeback is intelligent, loyal to its family, vigilant, and somewhat suspicious of strangers. It is said to have the heart of a lion, and is an excellent companion. It is a gentle dog but may be too big and rambunctious for small children. Like other hounds, it accepts other pets if introduced to them while a puppy.

Training: This breed is known to learn quickly, but due to its great strength and heritage, it may be a bit stubborn. A confident, experienced trainer is needed to work with this breed.

Basenji

Origin: The "barkless hound" is among the oldest known breeds in the world. It originated in the Congo and was transported very early to Egypt. *Basenji* means wild and violent in Swahili. When excited, instead of barking, this primitive breed chortles and yodels.

Aptitude: The Basenji is a hunting breed that is small but physically strong, with a possible hereditary susceptibility to distemper. It doesn't like inclement weather; it hates the rain and can't stand cold or drafty accommodations. This breed is inquisitive, clever, and stubborn. It trails by scent and sight.

Size: Males weigh 24 pounds (11 kg) and stand 17 inches (43 cm) tall. Females weigh 22 pounds (10 kg) and stand 16 inches (40 cm) tall.

Coat: This African breed's coat is short, dense, and fine.

Colors: Chestnut red and white, pure black and white, tricolor, brindle and white are all acceptable colors.

Coat care and exercise: Being short, the Basenji's coat is easily kept, brushing with a rubber currycomb or wiping with a chamois being the total requirement. This protective breed is ideal for apartment living, since it demands little exercise. If allowed the run of a large yard, it may become more active.

Attitude: The Basenji is a remarkable breed that is sometimes described as catlike due to its tendency to lick its coat and feet. This is an independent dog, one that bonds tightly with its master and needs human company. It is not a pet for children, and is rather reserved toward strangers. Basenjis tolerate other dogs fairly well, but must be introduced carefully to other family pets.

Training: Lacking obedience training, this primitive dog is quite headstrong. It likes to please, but trainers must have great patience and cunning to teach this dog.

Bloodhound

Origin: Belgium is usually considered the origin of this trail hound, although its roots may go back to ancient Greece and Rome. Its ancestors were probably the Saint Hubert's hound of eighth-century Belgium.

Aptitude: The Bloodhound may have been named for its ability to follow a wounded creature interminably, or it may have simply been short for pure-blooded. In either case, this animal has the best nose in the tracking business. It is happiest when trailing, but is usually fairly content to be a pet. It is perhaps the most determined tracker in exis-

Basenji.

tence, and is unequaled in stamina as well.

Size: Males weigh 90 pounds (41 kg) and stand 26 inches (66 cm) tall. Females weigh 80 pounds (36 kg) and stand 23 inches (66 cm) tall. This doesn't mean the dogs can't weigh more and stand taller, providing they remain in proportion.

Coat: The Bloodhound coat is short, smooth, and tight.

Colors: Black and tan, red and tan, and tawny are the usual colors of the Bloodhound, but they may also have badger-colored hair flecked with white. A small amount of white is allowed on the chest and feet.

Coat care and exercise: Grooming a Bloodhound is easily accomplished. A short bristled brush or

Bloodhound.

rubber slicker brush or currycomb are used to keep this dog glossy. Although puppies' exercise shouldn't be forced, as adults these dogs will outwalk most humans. They have phenomenal stamina when following any trail.

Attitude: The Bloodhound is people-oriented, gentle, and affectionate. It is an excellent children's dog, providing the children learn not to torment the dog. This dog will tolerate nearly any abuse without retribution. It is quite tolerant of other family pets, strangers, and visitors alike.

Training: Patience, tact, patience, consistency, and more patience are required to train a Bloodhound. It learns very early how to avoid training with its soulful eyes and countenance. It seems to believe obedience to commands is not required if it looks sad. If you own a Bloodhound and want to see it excel, look into formal tracking trials or search-and-rescue work.

Working Group

Rottweiler

Origin: The country of origin of this powerful dog is open to question. Named for the German town of Rottweil, where it was developed, it was used there as a drover, guard dog, companion, and draft dog to pull butchers' carts. The Rottweiler probably is a descendent of dogs that herded livestock over the Alps to feed Roman soldiers on their marches across Europe. It neared extinction before the turn of the century and was revived partly due to its adaptability as a police dog.

Aptitude: A very strong dog, the Rottweiler has many useful functions in today's society. It has a highly protective nature and is frequently the breed of choice when selecting a family companion and guard dog. Its great strength makes it valuable as a police dog, and it is often found in virtually all athletic canine competitions.

Size: These dogs weigh 90 to 110 pounds (41 to 50 kg) and males stand 24 to 27 inches (57 to 69 cm) tall. Females stand 22 to 25 inches (55 to 63 cm) tall.

Coat: The coat is flat, straight, coarse, dense, and of medium length. Its undercoat varies with climactic influences.

Colors: The Rottweiler's color is a uniform black with rust or mahogany markings.

Coat care and exercise: Grooming a Rottie is not much of a job. A rubber grooming glove is preferred over brushes, but a rubber currycomb also works well.

Exercise must be afforded this active working dog. Running is preferred by the dog, but any vigorous activity will serve to keep this dog fit and in good spirits. Swimming, agility work, and country runs are recommended.

Attitude: The Rottweiler is a loyal, intelligent, and obedient companion. It has strong family ties and is naturally quite protective. This dog is considered by many to be one of the bravest dogs there are. When introduced to children as a puppy, it will be a fine playmate. Adult Rottweilers are usually rather dominant toward other dogs. While their temperament is loving toward friends, they are extremely vigilant and assertive toward strangers.

Training: Puppy training is essential, and dominance training throughout life is advised. This breed needs a trainer who is calm and considerate, giving the dog plenty of praise when it performs correctly. It is a strong, dominant dog that responds best to consistent training, using a calm, reassuring tone of voice.

Rottweiler.

Boxer

Origin: The Boxer, as we know it, originated in Munich, Germany, about 1850. It was bred from Bulldogs and Mastiffs, and was used primarily as a pit fighter.

Aptitude: The Boxer is a working dog, and is best appreciated when given something to do. It has been used as a guide dog, and its intelligence lends it nicely to obedience trials and agility work. Used in Germany for police work, the Boxer obviously has a big heart and is quite trainable.

Size: Males weigh about 70 pounds (32 kg) and stand 22.5 to 25 inches (57 to 63 cm) tall. Females weigh about 60 pounds (27 kg) and stand 21 to 23.5 inches (54 to 60 cm) tall.

Coat: The Boxer's coat is short, lustrous, and lies close and tight to the body.

Colors: The breed standard calls for fawn and brindle colors. Fawn describes everything from light tan to mahogany; brindle includes defined black stripes to heavy stripes. White markings that do not exceed one third of the entire coat are permissible. White boxers are disqualified from showing.

Coat care and exercise: Grooming a Boxer is a simple job. Using a chamois or a rubber grooming mitten, the dog is rubbed down occasionally, and looks shiny and glossy.

Attitude: The Boxer, despite its pit heritage, is friendly to a fault. It is a spontaneous, happy, uncomplicated dog that makes a superb family pet. A sweet disposition and a lively nature make it a wonderful

Boxer.

children's companion and playmate. Although quite protective of its family members, the Boxer is easily trained to adjust to other pets as well. Sometimes almost boisterous, the Boxers will join you for a romp or a walk at any time of the day or night.

Training: Being a bubbly, happy dog, most training is geared to quiet the dog. The Boxer is desirous of pleasing its master, and training chores are happy times of interaction with your dog. It delights in obedience work, and is often engaged in agility trials.

Siberian Husky

Origin: Northeastern Asia produced this tireless sled dog. It was developed by the Chukchi people of Siberia as their only means of transportation.

Aptitude: A Siberian Husky's principal use is pulling a sled, generally as a member of a team of similar dogs. It has proven itself capable of fantastic feats of speed and endurance in that endeavor. Skijoring is another similar task in which the athletic, powerful, streamlined Husky excels.

Size: Males weigh 45 to 60 pounds (20 to 27 kg) and stand 21 to 23.5 inches (54 to 60 cm) tall. Females weigh 35 to 50 pounds (17.5 to 23 kg) and stand 20 to 22 inches (58 to 55 cm) tall.

Coat: A true double coat keeps the Siberian warm in arctic weather. It is of medium length, and the undercoat is soft and dense, while the guard hairs are straight, and lie smooth.

Colors: All colors from solid black to pure white are permissible. Many striking markings abound to adorn the beautiful lines of the Siberian.

Coat care and exercise: The coat of this breed requires little regular care in spite of its density. Its beauty is greatest when the dog is kept outdoors, when the weather is cold. Grooming is advised during the semiannual shedding.

Like other working dogs, the Siberian thrives on exercise, and to make one settle for less is a crime. Melancholy, boredom, bad habits, and howling are usual signs that the Husky isn't exercised strenuously and regularly enough.

Attitude: The Siberian is a friendly, cheerful dog, playful and affectionate. It has been bred to serve as a sled dog, and in human environments it is often a mischievous, independent thinker that is prone to wander off. It accepts other dogs if introduced properly, but is often a threat to cats and small pets.

Not usually considered to be a strict family or apartment pet, the Siberian Husky likes children, but would rather go for a run over the mountainside than play in a backyard.

Training: Many Siberians are obstinate and difficult to train. Consistency and patience is required of a Husky trainer. Although clever, this dog would rather make up its own behavior rules than accept those of its human owners.

Siberian Husky.

Doberman Pinscher

Origin: Taxes weigh heavily in the origin of the Doberman Pinscher. This breed was developed in Apolda, Thuringen, Germany, in about 1880 by a door-to-door tax collector. As you might guess, Ludwig Dobermann wasn't a very popular gent, and he developed the breed to protect him from robbers and disgruntled taxpayers. The Dobie's progenitors include the Rottweiler, German Shepherd, German Pinscher, and Manchester Terrier.

Aptitude: This breed has strong protective tendencies and is well suited as a companion and defense dog. Once quite aggressive, the Dobie's temperament has been somewhat remodeled to produce a more refined guardian and courageous pet, while retaining its intelligence and trainability.

Doberman Pinscher.

Coat care and exercise: The sleek coat requires little care except for regular wiping with a chamois or rubber grooming mitt.

Exercise is important to the happiness and well-being of this working dog. The Dobie wants regular running, swimming, or other strenuous activity. It may adapt to apartment living, but will do much better in an active, outdoor, athletic family.

Attitude: A Doberman Pinscher is a clean, cunning, brave, intelligent companion that bonds well with its owner and family. It is a dog with tremendous stamina and athletic ability. Its temperament is happy and carefree, but unrecognized visitors often are stopped in their tracks merely by the appearance of the resident Doberman.

Training: Training this streamlined, strong breed requires special attention. If Dobies are not correctly handled as puppies, they may become neurotic and untrustworthy. Their training must be attended with utmost care. Consistency, ample praise when performing well, and absolutely no force is most likely to get positive results with training.

Akita

Origin: Not only did the Akita originate in Japan, it is designated as a national monument in that country. It was bred originally by exiled nobility as a hunting dog, used later as a fighter, and in its long and colorful history has even been served as a menu item. Although lit-

The intelligence, athletic ability, and attitude of this breed is well suited to obedience work and competition in agility trials.

Size: Males weigh about 80 pounds (36 kg) and stand 26 to 28 inches (66 to 71 cm) tall. Females weigh about 65 pounds (29 kg) and stand 24 to 26 inches (61 to 66 cm) tall.

Coat: The smooth-haired, short, hard coat of the Doberman lays close to its body.

Colors: Black with rust points is the most common color seen, but the dog is also seen sporting a red coat, blue, and fawn or Isabella (a fawn or light bay color). All have the same rust accents.

tle is said of its ancestors, it is probably of Spitz lineage.

Aptitude: Today, the noble Akita is primarily a family pet and guardian, although occasionally seen in a sled team. It is well adapted to serve as a watch dog with no specific guard training.

Size: Males weigh up to 110 pounds (50 kg) and stand 26 to 28 inches (66 to 71 cm) tall. Females weigh about 85 pounds (38 kg) and stand 24 to 26 inches (61 to 66 cm) tall.

Coat: A thick, soft, dense undercoat lies under guard hair that is straight and harsh. This double coat is longer on the body and tail than on the appendages.

Colors: Virtually any color is allowed from pure white to very dark. Brindles and pintos are common, and well-balanced, clear patches or markings add greatly to the Akita beauty.

Coat care and exercise: Care for the dense Akita coat is straightforward and simple. Semiannual shedding usually requires extensive brushing and combing; in-between times, very little brushing is needed.

Exercise must be included in your Akita ownership. These dogs are from hardy hunting dog stock, and they need their share of physical and mental activity.

Attitude: The Akita is an intelligent, relatively obedient pet, impassive and reserved. It is even-tempered, but often independent. It usually is quite dominant around other dogs, especially those of their own sex. Cats

Akita.

and other small pets are at risk, and should be introduced early in the life of an Akita. Children of the family are accepted, but neighborhood children are often excluded from the Akita circle of close friends.

Training: Trainers should be experienced and should approach Akita training slowly, with consistency and confidence. This intelligent animal won't tolerate abuse or strong-arm techniques, and once it rebels, you have a real problem on your hands. Home training should begin early in the life of an Akita puppy, and continued indefinitely.

Great Dane

Origin: Known in its native Germany as Deutsche Dogge or German Boarhound, this majestic dog has the blood of other grand breeds flowing through its veins. Some references list the English Mastiff and Greyhound as its progenitors; others name the Irish Wolfhound as the principal ancestor.

Aptitude: Developed as a hunter of savage wild boars, one would expect this dog to be rough, undisciplined, and untrustworthy; nothing is further from the truth. The Great Dane is an excellent watchdog (who would be foolish enough to test one?) and family companion.

Size: Most males weigh well over 100 pounds (45 kg) and stand more than 30 inches (76 cm) tall. Females are correspondingly hefty and stand no less than 28 inches (71 cm) tall.

Great Dane.

Coat: The Dane's coat is short, thick, and glossy.

Colors: Acceptable Great Dane colors are brindle, golden fawn, steel blue, black, and harlequin. Harlequin Danes are white with fairly small, irregular black patches well distributed over the body.

Coat care and exercise: Great Dane coats are easily maintained by grooming several times weekly with a chamois or rubber currycomb.

Definitely not an apartment dog, this giant requires a significant amount of exercise to stay fit. It prefers to run free on woodland trails when possible.

Attitude: The Dane is an affectionate, calm, distinguished creature, displaying both sensitivity and intelligence. Not quarrelsome, it is sometimes uncertain of strangers, but it quickly accepts guests when introduced. Its reputation is well deserved for getting along with other household pets, and dogs of any size. Children raised in a family that owns a Great Dane have no need to worry about anything except being stepped on by this friendly giant.

Training: Giant breeds mature quickly into big, ungainly animals that are difficult to handle. For this reason, training diligence is necessary when Danes are puppies. This breed responds well to quiet handling and consistent techniques. Nagging and raising your voice will defeat you as quickly as anything. When training to the lead, consider the size of your Dane when it is fully grown!

Saint Bernard

Origin: Developed from the heavy Asian Molosser that was brought into Switzerland by Roman armies, the Saint Bernard is the product of a famous hospice in the Swiss Alps. The Archdeacon Bernard de Menthon lent his name to this dog that was bred and maintained specifically for alpine rescue work.

Aptitude: Although this giant was well suited for finding trails in the snowy Alps, it is rarely so used today. It is often hitched to a cart in a parade, or decorated with blankets, first aid kits, and the ever-present flask on the breast strap of its harness. Today, the good-humored dog lives as a well-loved pet and family companion.

Size: Males weigh well over 100 pounds (45 kg) and stand at least 27.5 inches (70 cm) tall. Females stand 25 inches (63 cm) tall.

Coat: The Saint Bernard's coat is very dense, smooth, tough, and relatively short.

Colors: The Saint Bernard is white with red, or red with white. Red and brown with brindle patches are the characteristic colors of this giant. White is always a part of the Saint Bernard, but all white is not allowed.

Coat care and exercise: Extensive grooming is necessary to keep the Saint Bernard's coat in top shape. Combing and brushing daily are advised.

Exercise is easier to handle, since the giant's need is somewhat less than other working dogs. Young Saints frolic and play to get their exercise, and older dogs will accept a few turns around the block a couple of times daily.

Attitude: This friendly dog is right at home with children, and household pets rarely cause any problem. The temperament and social behavior is exemplary if training is given early. The Saint has a sense of humor that belies its huge body. Its bark is sufficient warning to ward off unwanted interlopers, but its bark is probably worse than its bite.

Training: All giant breeds should receive some obedience training when puppies; this is true of Saints as well. Easily trained with consistency and appreciation for tasks correctly accomplished, praise should be awarded regularly.

Saint Bernard.

Terrier Group

Miniature Schnauzer

Origin: A German terrier of small stature, this hardy little dog was bred from Standard Schnauzers that were crossed with Affenpinschers and possibly Poodles. It has little common heritage with other terriers.

Aptitude: This dog was a farm resident in Germany and was used to kill rats and other small rodents. It is a happy, robust little dog that is always ready for a romp. The Miniature Schnauzer is a fine children's pet, and as such enjoys wide acceptance as a tough family companion.

Size: Although the breed standard lists no weight range, both sexes of this breed stand 12 to 14 inches (31 to 36 cm) and weigh about 13 to 15 pounds (6 to 7 kg).

Miniature Schnauzers.

Coat: A close undercoat is found under the Miniature Schnauzer's hard, wiry outer hair. Coats that are too soft or smooth are considered faults.

Colors: These beautiful dogs appear in one of three colors: salt-and-pepper, black and silver, and solid black. The salt-and-pepper color is the result of black and white banded hairs and solid black and white hairs. A slight tan shading is allowed in this color.

Coat care and exercise: Plucking is necessary to maintain the Schnauzer's coat, and a show dog must never be clipped. Professional stripping every six to eight weeks is required if the dog is kept in show condition; however, many owners learn to groom their own pets with scissors and a clipper. The results are not as classic, but the expense is far less.

Having enormous energy, the Miniature Schnauzer requires an abundance of exercise. In addition to playing with children, this dog should be taken for regular runs in the park or fast walks about the neighborhood.

Attitude: This dog is lively, intelligent, and clever, but it can be stubborn if improperly handled. It has great loyalty to its family and is an above-average watchdog. It has a tendency to bark when surprised or when bored and has too little to do. It usually adapts well to other family pets but pet rodents should be carefully guarded from a Schnauzer.

Training: When treated fairly, the Miniature Schnauzer is a willing, biddable dog. Consistency is important when teaching it, and on occasion it will display its active imagination when interpreting your command.

West Highland White Terrier

Origin: Poltalloch, Scotland, is designated as the place where the West Highland White Terrier originated. Historically, this dog has been known as the Poltalloch Terrier and Roseneath Terrier.

Aptitude: This dog is best suited as a family companion with its share of Scottish spunk and determination. Equally at home in its yard or an apartment, this hardy terrier is a playful children's pet.

Size: As with several other terriers, there is no weight listed in the official breed standard. Males stand 11 inches (28 cm) tall; bitches stand 10 inches (25 cm).

Coat: The Westie has a thick double coat made up of straight, hard guard hairs and a shorter, softer undercoat.

Colors: All Westies are solid white or solid heavy wheaten.

Coat care and exercise: Regular plucking is required to maintain a Westie's show coat. Pet owners often trim their Westies with clippers and scissors to save expense.

This little terrier loves to play ball, romp, and frolic with its children. Its instinct to dig often gets it in trouble, but its mischievous looks usually bail it out.

Attitude: The Westie is a fearlessly alert, loyal, and vigilant watchdog. It thrives on play, but is quite self-confident and not easily impressed. It is a loving but cunning little dog, stubborn at times, and ingenious all of the time. It is hardy and usually gets along fine with other dogs and children, but it has a dominant streak that sometimes shows up around other dogs. If introduced as a youth to cats, it may tolerate them, but felines are great sources of entertainment and exercise for most Westies.

Training: This little terrier often presents problems for its owners in the training department. It's not a lack of intelligence but rather an abundance of it that causes most of the difficulty. It needs firm, straightforward training, beginning when it is a puppy. Persistence and consistency will win out, providing the handler can get past its cute face.

West Highland White Terrier.

Cairn Terrier

Origin: Indigenous to the Isle of Skye in the highlands of northwest Scotland, the Cairn was named for the stone markers called *cairns* that grace that land. These fierce but diminutive hunters claim common origin with Westies and other terriers of Scotland.

Aptitude: Originally bred to burrow into holes in the rough stone cairns to eradicate rats and otters, the Cairn maintains some of this tenacity. In the absence of stony cairns, it is a valuable house pet and children's companion.

Size: Males weigh 14 pounds (6.3 kg) and stand 10 inches (25 cm) tall. Bitches weigh 13 pounds (6 kg) and stand 9.5 inches (24 cm) tall.

Coat: Cairn coats are double, hard, and weather-resistant. The guard hairs are profuse, covering a soft furry undercoat.

Colors: Any color except white is allowed.

Cairn Terrier.

Coat care and exercise: Plucking twice a year will keep the coat in show shape, providing it is combed and brushed three times a week. Pet owners can learn to groom their Cairn with clippers if desired.

A typical terrier, the Cairn is virtually bursting with energy and needs plenty of exercise. A big yard and children to play with will help, but supplement this exercise with regular walks or runs in the park.

Attitude: A brave, cheerful extrovert, this dog is quite affectionate and playful. It is eager to please, and a vigilant watchdog that may surprise interlopers. Its temperament is uncomplicated; it makes a wonderful children's companion and can tolerate rough play. It has a great sense of humor and gets along fairly well with other dogs. Rodent pets may be at risk, and cats should be introduced to the Cairn while it is still a puppy.

Training: Early training is needed in this terrier, especially when playing. Tug-of-war games may get out of hand if not closely controlled. The biggest mistake owners make when they train this dog is allowing it to get away with doing the wrong thing. As is always the case, consistency and persistence will win the day.

Scottish Terrier

Origin: Aberdeen, Scotland, is the site of origin of the Scottie; in fact, it was once called the Aberdeen Terrier. This tough little terrier is related to others that have their origin in the rocky Scottish highlands.

Aptitude: The Scottie was bred to hunt foxes, rabbits, and weasels and drag them from their burrows. It is noted for its tenacity, fearlessness, and feisty nature. Often a one-person dog, this terrier is devoted to its family, and acts boldly around strangers.

Size: Either sex should weigh 18 to 22 pounds (8 to 10 kg) and stand about 10 inches (25.4 cm).

Coat: Scottie coats are short, double, dense, and intensely hard and wiry.

Colors: Steel or iron gray, brindled or grizzled, black, sandy, or wheaten are the allowable colors.

Coat care and exercise: The wiry coat should be hand-plucked by a professional groomer twice a year to maintain show quality; in between, the hair should be regularly groomed by comb and brush.

The Scottie is somewhat adaptable to the family lifestyle. It is an active dog, but will usually settle for modest exercise. Walks are always appreciated, and this dog's hardiness allows for extensive exercise when possible.

Attitude: The Scottish Terrier is a sober, vigilant watchdog, and becomes quite attached to its family members. It is a noble creature with a mind of its own. Its temperament is even and predictable, and it gets along well with other household pets as well as with other dogs. Children must learn to respect this dog's domain.

Scottish Terrier.

Training: The Scottie is an aristocrat. It is an independent little dog that thinks it is much bigger than it is. Training needs to be approached with that in mind. Give it respect and consistency and it will reward you with obedience.

Fox Terrier, Wire

Origin: Of ancient lineage, the Wirehaired Fox Terrier probably traces its ancestry to Wales, although it was shown as a variety of the Smooth-Coated Fox Terrier for many years. The two breeds were interbred for many years as well.

Aptitude: This breed was originally classed with the sporting dogs, since it was specifically bred to *go to ground* and pull foxes and badgers from their burrows. Today, Fox Terriers are kept as family pets and companions.

Size: Wirehaired Fox Terriers weigh about 18 pounds (8 kg) and

Fox Terrier, WIre.

stand no more than 15.5 inches (39 cm) tall. Females usually weigh 16 pounds (7 kg) and are proportionately smaller.

Coat: The coat of a Wirehair appears twisted, broken, or wiry, like coconut matting. It is a double coat with soft, finer hair under the twisted guard hair.

Colors: Predominate white is required, with patches of any color except brindle, red, liver, or slate blue. These colors are objectionable, although not disqualifications.

Coat care and exercise: Hand plucking is required to maintain a show coat, but this is often forsaken by pet owners who groom their dogs with clippers and scissors. Combing and brushing several times weekly is also needed to keep the coat clean and in good condition.

Exercise is important in this energetic, active dog. If exercise is neglected, the dog will often become melancholy and bored, and will develop barking, digging, or other bad habits.

Attitude: The Wirehaired Fox Terrier is a wonderful children's pet. Its intelligence makes it a clever playmate, and most are blessed with a great sense of humor. A cheerful, happy dog, this dog, nevertheless, is prone to dominate others of its kind. It is known to attack threatening dogs, but is friendly to strangers.

Training: Quick to learn, the Wirehair is usually quite easily trained although it might have a stubborn streak. Begin training fundamentals early, and stay consistent in all teaching.

Airedale Terrier

Origin: This tallest terrier traces its ancestry to Yorkshire, England, where it was bred from Old English Terriers and Otterhounds. It has been known as Bingley or Waterside Terrier.

Aptitude: Originally used for hunting birds, foxes, otters, and other small game, this terrier retains some of its hunting ability, but is kept mainly as a companion.

Size: The Airedale's weight isn't listed in the breed standard, but they usually weigh about 45 pounds (20 kg). Males stand about 23 inches (58 cm), bitches slightly less.

Coat: Airedale coats are dense, hard, wiry, lying straight and close. It has a short undercoat of softer hair.

Colors: This dog is basically tan, with darker shadings and a black or dark grizzle-colored saddle.

Coat care and exercise: For showing, the dog needs plucking regularly, but for routine pet care, much less is required. Many Airedale owners groom their dogs with scissors and clippers every three months.

The exercise demand is about average for medium-build dogs. Regular play periods, romping with children, and a few trips around the block on a leash will satisfy most. The Airedale is a great swimmer and ball player, and most will retrieve balls without training.

Airedale Terrier.

Attitude: This breed is notoriously tough, loyal, intelligent, and resolute. An excellent family pet, the Airedale is playful and patient with children, and full of fun. It makes a good watchdog and is quite adept at dog sports. It is rather dominant toward other dogs, but this tendency can usually be managed with training.

Training: The Airedale is biddable, bright, and easily trained if patience and consistency is practiced. It often responds best to very short training sessions that include several different exercises. It sometimes shows stubbornness when commands are repeated time and again.

Soft Coated Wheaten Terrier

Origin: Ireland is the land of the Soft Coated Wheaten, where it was an ancestor of the Kerry Blue Terrier.

Aptitude: In its native land, many years ago, it served as a hunter of small game, a drover of livestock, and a courageous watchdog and companion. It was a midsized Irish farm dog that has become a fine dog sport competitor. It is well suited for Frisbee and agility contests, and does well at obedience.

Size: Males weigh 35 to 40 pounds (16 to 18 kg) and stand 18 to 19 inches (45 to 48 cm) tall. Females weigh 30 to 35 pounds (14 to 16 kg) and stand 17 to 18 inches (43 to 45 cm) tall.

Coat: The coat of the Soft Coated Wheaten distinguishes it from all other terriers. It has a single coat of soft, silky texture with gentle waves; however, it isn't wooly or cottony.

Colors: Colors may be summed up as any shade of wheaten, the pale yellow color of wheat. White is a major fault.

Coat care and exercise: This breed's soft coat requires no clipping or plucking, but must be combed frequently to keep it free of tangles. Some pet owners prefer to cut the coat with shears or clippers to avoid tangles and burrs.

An active, energetic dog, the Wheaten needs the opportunity to burn off its calories in exercise. It makes an excellent apartment pet when taken for routine walks around the block and a romp in the park every day.

Attitude: The Wheaten is an extrovert, playful and active, eager to learn and ready for fun. It bonds with its family, is self-confident and loving, especially with children. It accepts other household pets if it is introduced to them when a puppy, and will usually accept cats.

Soft Coated Wheaten Terriers.

Training: Because of its intelligence, this dog does well with training. Quick to learn, and quite biddable, it should be taught manners when weaned, and is usually ready for obedience training by the time it is a few months old.

Toy Group

Pomeranian

Origin: This diminutive, fashionable toy derived its name from Pomerania, Germany, although this probably isn't where the breed originated. Bred from arctic Spitz-type sled dogs, similar to the Chow Chow, Norwegian Elkhound, and Samoyed, the Pomeranian is a man-made creation. The site of the most concentrated miniaturization of these dogs to produce the present-day Pomeranian was apparently Pomerania, a former province of Prussia. The breed's most likely progenitor was the German Deutscher Spitz. Poms weren't called Pomeranians until they arrived in England.

Aptitude: Having its heritage in herding dogs and hard-working sled dogs, this little dog often thinks it is much larger than it is, much to its dismay. Today, the Pomeranian serves humans in the most useful and pleasurable role possible: It is a lively companion, a vigilant pet, a delightful lapdog of the highest quality. Only an average children's pet, this tiny dog is probably nervous or cautious around the smaller family members. Once the fear of being stepped on or dropped is overcome, it usually reciprocates the love of children.

Size: The Pomeranian ideal size is from 4 to 5 pounds (1.8 to 2.3 kg), although it may be exhibited from 3 to 7 pounds (1.4 to 3.1 kg).

Coat: Retaining some of its sled dog identification, the Pomeranian sports a double coat, its short, soft undercoat being covered with a longer, coarse, guard coat. Its feathering is copious on legs, tail, and lower body.

Colors: Poms may be shown by color in three classes: red, orange, cream and sable; black, brown and blue; any other allowed color. Each color is well identified by the breed standard.

Coat care and exercise: A significant amount of time must be devoted to grooming this dog's coat, every day or several times weekly. It is combed with a coarse comb, and brushed lightly, leaving the soft undercoat intact.

Exercise demanded by this tiny dog is quite minimal, but the breed is normally a hardy one, and the Pom has amazing stamina for long walks and runs in the park.

Attitude: This intelligent, agile, and cheerful little dog is eager to please and loyal to its family. Sometimes displaying a bravery that exceeds good sense, the Pom may attack much larger dogs when it feels threatened. Usually, it gets on fairly well with dogs and other

Pomeranian.

household pets. It has a sweet, engaging temperament, but does not often cling to its owners.

Training: The Pomeranian is a great student, and can be trained to do amazing feats in addition to the usual dog obedience and good manners. It is quick to learn and highly intelligent.

Chihuahua

Origin: Sometime around the ninth century, the Toltec peoples of Mexico raised little dogs called Techichi, which may have originated in Central America prior to the fifth century in the Mayan culture. Chihuahuas trace their lineage to these dogs that may have been a part of religious ceremonies. Its name is taken from the state of Chihuahua, Mexico.

Chihuahua.

Aptitude: The Chihuahua is recognized as the smallest dog breed in the world, and like other toys, it occupies a favored position in families. It doesn't pull draft carts, rescue drowning fishermen, or retrieve ducks in frigid waters. It is a pet, a lapdog of the finest variety, and it isn't ashamed of this designation.

Size: This breed, male or female, must weigh less than 6 pounds (2.7 kg).

Coat: Two coat varieties are recognized. The Smooth Coat has soft hair that grows close. The Long Coats are also of a soft texture, flat or slightly curly with an undercoat.

Colors: Any color is permissible, solid, marked, or splashed.

Coat care and exercise: The longhaired variety should be brushed and combed frequently, and the smoothhaired variety should be occasionally groomed with a rubber mitt or short-bristled brush.

This tiny dog will get sufficient exercise indoors to satisfy its needs, although most enjoy a walk around the block or a jaunt in the park.

Attitude: This dog is an intelligent, playful pet, sensitive to voice modulations, and quite sociable with other pets of all sizes. In this regard, it must be protected from larger household dogs. It can be stubborn, and show an unexpected independent nature. Being so tiny, it isn't suitable for small children who might inadvertently step on or drop it.

Training: Because it can cause little damage, its training is often neglected. This dog is often trained to use a litter pan, much like a cat, which is a shame, because in spite of its diminutive size, it *is* a dog, with all the needs of other canines. It actually has a biddable nature and accepts training of all types, including obedience. It is a better companion if it is treated and trained like a dog.

Yorkshire Terrier

Origin: Along with a wide array of dogs, including Waterside, Maltese, Manchester, and Skye Terriers in its lineage, the Yorkshire Terrier originated in the West Riding region of Yorkshire, England. Coal miners and weavers developed the breed during Victorian times to serve as ratters and catchers of vermin of all sorts.

Aptitude: Although bred to kill vermin, this dog has become a status symbol, and is usually considered a pampered pet. Being such a small dog, it often suffers at the hands of children, and commonly will react in a reserved fashion when approached by them.

Size: In dog shows, the Yorkies' weight must not exceed 7 pounds (3.2 kg).

Coat: A glossy, fine, silky coat graces the Yorkie from stem to stern. The coat is long and perfectly straight, and is usually trimmed to floor length. Its cranial coiffure usually is managed with a single bow or pair of bows.

Colors: Two adult colors are recognized: a dark steel-blue, not silvery, and not mingled with fawn, bronze, or black hair; and tan, in which the dark tan hair is shaded to lighter hues toward the end. Tan coats have no black hair intermingled.

Coat care and exercise: Daily, concentrated grooming accompanies ownership of this beautiful little dog. This is always a limiting factor in obtaining the breed. Although it seems a shame to cut off this lovely coat, many people refuse to be a slave to dog grooming, while still enjoying the personality of the Yorkie. They have the coat reduced to a manageable inch-long (2.5-cm) stubble, and both dog and owner seem perfectly happy.

This breed adapts well to apartment living and usually fills its exercise needs by running around on the floor. This doesn't address the other benefits of outdoor exercise such as fresh air, new smells, and social contact with other dogs and humans.

Attitude: This lively, intelligent, and brave little dog bonds tightly with its family. A fun-loving pet, it is very alert, and its barking often ranks it high on the list of early warning devices. It is braver than necessary around other dogs, and may even courageously challenge them. As with other toy breeds, it is often frightened by small children, but older children are great playmates and pals. Cats usually are accepted friends, and commonly play with Yorkies, but pet rodents are at risk when exposed to them.

Training: Training is often neglected in this quick-witted breed because of its beautiful, sculptured appearance and somewhat stubborn attitude. However, if you have patience and apply a consistent approach, the Yorkie's intelligence will reward you with a rare commodity: a well-trained Yorkshire Terrier.

Yorkshire Terrier.

Shih Tzu

Origin: This breed's flowing coat contributes about the only similarity to its namesake, the lion. It originated in the Buddhist temples of the Tang Dynasty in Beijing, China, more than 1,000 years ago. Probably bred from miniature Chinese dogs crossed with Tibetan breeds, the Shih Tzu was a great favorite of Chinese emperors.

Aptitude: Bred to be a companion to courtiers and nobility, this dog is among everyone's favorites today because of its ability to bring humor, gentleness, and vivacity to any home. As a puppy it is a bundle of energy that loves children. As an adult, it is a dignified member of the family.

Size: Shih Tzus weigh 9 to 16 pounds (4 to 7 kg) and stand 9 to 10.5 inches (23 to 25 cm) tall.

Shih Tzu.

Coat: Shih Tzus sport a long and flowing double coat that is dense and slightly wavy.

Colors: All colors and combinations of colors are permissible, and there are no color disqualifications.

Coat care and exercise: Dogs of this breed require a significant amount of grooming; tangles can be prevented only by daily combing. Hair can be kept from the dog's tender eyes by a ribbon, a factor that sometimes discourages potential owners; others deal with the long hair with scissors and clippers. The personality of this dog doesn't seem to be affected by wearing a bobbed-off coat.

Exercise is easily taken care of with regular short walks or romps in the backyard or park.

Attitude: Affectionate, lovable, cheerful, and sociable seems to describe this dog's temperament. The Shih Tzu is usually an independent thinker that doesn't always accept every person as a friend, yet is loyal and devoted to its family. It usually accepts other dogs and household pets at face value. Children often appreciate this dog as a loving friend and playmate, and the dog returns this love many times over.

Training: The Shih Tzu's independent temperament often discourages owners from training, but when approached with respect and consistency, training efforts will pay off. The dog's intelligence and eagerness to please should be used as training tools.

Maltese

Origin: Having the distinction of being the most ancient of European toy breeds, the Maltese is also one of the oldest breeds known to man. The Italian island of Malta was visited by Phoenician traders who probably introduced this dog or its immediate ancestors to Malta. Greek writings dating to 300 B.C. mentioned dogs of this type. Publius, the Roman governor of Malta, owned a Maltese at the time of the Apostle Paul in 38 A.D.

Aptitude: This breed is, as it always has been, a cherished family pet. It has lived with nobility and the common folk for centuries with no other job than being a companion and friend.

Size: Either sex of this breed must weigh less than 7 pounds (3 kg), preferably in the range of 4 to 6 pounds (1.8 to 2.7 kg).

Coat: This tiny breed has a single silken coat that hangs long, flat, and flowing over the sides of its body to the floor.

Colors: The Maltese is pure white. Light tan or lemon-colored ears are permissible but not desirable.

Coat care and exercise: Grooming of the Maltese is a substantial endeavor as its silky coat requires daily brushing and combing. Like other toy breeds with similar coats, this tedious coat care problem is solved by pet owners with their clippers and shears.

The Maltese is content with the exercise it gets in the apartment or backyard, but it loves long walks

Maltese.

and the socialization it receives on a leash.

Attitude: A friendly, lovable, playful dog, the Maltese is eager to learn, a sensitive companion, and quite at home with older children who respect its size. A secure bond is formed with its owners, and the Maltese will go out of its way to avoid confrontations with other pets and people. It rarely barks, and can't be considered a watchdog by any stretch of the imagination.

Training: Providing a harsh voice and inconsistency are avoided, this sensitive, people-pleasing dog is relatively easily trained. It loves its family, is ready to obey, and appreciates any tokens offered for lessons learned. Don't let this dog's size, lovable nature, and cute appearance interfere with its training.

Miniature Pinscher

Origin: The Miniature Pinscher predates the Doberman Pinscher by a few centuries, and is not, therefore, a downsize of the popular Dobie. They do share origins, both having been developed in Germany. The principal ancestor of the Min Pin was probably the Klein Pinscher from Scandinavia.

Aptitude: Miniature Pinschers are really terriers and were developed to corner and kill rats and other vermin. As is often the case, the Min Pin has evolved as a companion animal and watchdog.

Size: Min Pins of both sexes stand 10 to 12.5 inches (25.4 to 31 cm) tall, and are disqualified if under 10 inches.

Coat: This breed has a close-adhering coat that is smooth, hard, short, straight, and lustrous.

Miniature Pinscher.

Colors: Several colors are permissible: solid clear red, stag red (intermingling black hairs), black with rust markings, and chocolate with rust markings.

Coat care and exercise: The coat of a Min Pin requires very little grooming. A chamois cloth or rubber grooming mitt is used for routine care.

Attitude: The lively Min Pin is a vigilant watchdog that barks its alarm. Highly intelligent, this courageous dog is dependent, loyal, and often suspicious of strangers. It is usually considered somber, but the temperament depends somewhat on early training. It is not considered the best children's dog, but that depends on the age of the children. It accepts cats and other pets fairly well.

Training: The Min Pin's intelligent and biddable nature makes it highly trainable. Quick to learn and obey, this little dog wants to please and thrives on being kept busy. Its jumping ability, cleverness, and problem-solving capacity should make agility trials and obedience work a snap.

Pug

Origin: Pugs have several other names including *Carlin* in France, *Mopshond* in Holland, *Mops* in Germany, and *Dutch Pug* or *Chinese Pug* in England. The breed probably originated in the Orient, most likely in Tibet or China. It was carried first to the Netherlands, then to England where it further developed into its present form. The breed is reported to have Mastiffs in its ancestry, and bears a certain resemblance to the English Mastiff.

Aptitude: As is the case with many Oriental breeds, the Pug has always been principally a companion. It has served nobility in China and Holland, but was never known to earn its keep with a specific vocation.

Size: Pugs weigh 14 to 18 pounds (6.3 to 8 kg) and are proportionately built to retain their cobby stature.

Coat: The Pug coat is fine, smooth, soft, short, and glossy.

Colors: Permissible colors are silver, apricot-fawn, or black. All Pugs have a black mask.

Coat care and exercise: Best groomed with a rubber currycomb or grooming mitt, the Pug coat needs regular attention to prevent shedding on furniture.

Exercise usually consists of romps in the yard, walks around the neighborhood, or a run in the park. Take care to minimize outside activities in the hot summer.

Attitude: This calm, unobtrusive dog has a great sense of humor and loves to do tricks. It is affectionate toward children, and is always on its best behavior. Superb intelligence is another trait and it accepts cats and other small pets without question.

Training: The Pug is a people pleaser. It is a biddable quick learner that will amaze you with its comprehension. Often, this little dog will learn commands almost without explanation. Because the Pug is

Pug.

quite sensitive, it must be trained gently and with consistency. It can be severely disciplined by voice modulations, and care must be taken not to verbally abuse it.

Non-Sporting Group

Poodle

Origin: This breed originated in Germany (although some references put its origin in Russia), where it was a water retriever, as its German name *Pfudel* (splash in the water) denotes. Without its hairy disguise, it is a dead ringer for the Irish Water Spaniel or Rough-haired Water Dog of England. It migrated to France where it became immensely popular, hence the nickname *French Poodle*.

Aptitude: In its earlier days, the Poodle was involved with herding and water retrieving, and served as a military dog, guide dog, cart dog, and circus performer.

Size: Poodles are shown in three sizes: Standard Poodles stand more than 15 inches (38 cm) tall. Miniature Poodles stand 15 inches tall or less, but more than 10 inches (26 cm); Toy Poodles stand 10 inches (26 cm) tall or less.

Coat: The coat of a Poodle is curly, harsh, and dense. This breed may be shown in a number of different stylish clips or in its natural *corded* state.

Colors: The most important factor relates to the uniformity of solid color at the skin. Poodles appear in various tones and shades, including black, blue, gray, silver, brown, café-au-lait, apricot, cream, and white.

Coat care and exercise: To keep a Poodle in show condition, its coat requires constant attention; daily combing and brushing is needed. Most owner-handlers clip and scissor their dogs, but for the rest of us, professional groomers take on this responsibility. Pet Poodle owners may either clip their dogs closely at home, or pay a grooming shop to perform the task.

Standard and Miniature Poodles require significant exercise for good health. Having retained some of their inherited retrieving skills, they love to play ball and join in other dog sports.

Attitude: The Poodle is a lively, playful dog with intelligence to spare. It is sensitive, quick to learn, and appreciative of rewards. Standards are a bit more reserved than Miniatures. This breed is sociable and accepts children's attention and the society of other pets without trouble. They are fine watchdogs, but Miniatures and Toys are usually content to announce, whereas Standards are more likely to make their presence known to strangers.

Training: Standard and Miniature Poodles are biddable, eager-to-please dogs that can be taught to do practically anything. Toys are no less trainable, but most owners don't feel the need to train them. These dogs learn so quickly they often place high in agility trials, obedience contests, fly ball, and other participation dog sports.

Poodle.

Dalmatian

Origin: The ancient origin of this breed is open to conjecture. Some researchers claim that the breed came originally from western Yugoslavia, in the region of Dalmatia, which was once a province of Austria located on the Adriatic Sea north of Albania. The dog is traced into antiquity, and has been associated with a number of names. The English called it English Coach Dog, Carriage Dog, Plum Pudding Dog, Firehouse Dog, and the Spotted Dick.

Aptitude: This versatile dog has served in many capacities. It has been a war dog, draft dog, circus performing dog, shepherd, vermin hunter, firehouse mascot, bird dog, trail hound, and retriever, and in packs was used to hunt boar and stag. It formerly ran under Egyptian chariots, and later was a follower and guardian for horsemen. In more recent years, the Dalmatian has become a movie star in addition to its other accomplishments.

Size: Dogs and bitches stand 19 to 23 inches (48 to 58 cm) tall.

Coat: The Dalmatian coat is short, dense, fine, and close-fitting. It is neither silky nor wooly, but is glossy and sleek.

Colors: The ground color is pure white; spotting is either black or liver-colored. Other colors are not allowed. Dalmatians' spots are roundish, distinct, and range from the size of a dime to a half-dollar.

Coat care and exercise: The slick coat of a Dalmatian requires little care, but should be groomed daily

Dalmatian.

to eliminate unwanted hair on the rugs and furniture. Best groomed with a rubber currycomb or mitt, a chamois also serves quite well.

While the Dalmatian is adaptable to most situations, its exercise must not be overlooked. This is an active dog that delights in long walks, swims, and running in the park, and is a willing participant in dog sports. Unexercised Dalmatians will usually develop vices such as barking, fence running, digging, chewing, and other bad habits.

Attitude: The Dalmatian is often described as a high-sprited dog with tremendous stamina. It is a friendly, affectionate, clever, intelligent pet. It is a wonderful companion for children, perhaps a bit boisterous for toddlers, but a willing playmate for children of all ages. It is even-tempered, and accepts other household pets with little problem. Sometimes having the reputation of an expert guard dog, much of this tendency relates to training.

Training: As its heritage reflects, the Dalmatian can be taught to do just about anything. A quick and easy learner, it will readily respond to praise and reward, and has an excellent memory. Training is usually quite easy when you make your commands simple and plain, and when you are consistent in your technique.

Boston Terrier.

Boston Terrier

Origin: The United States is the origin of this breed, but both its parents came from England. In Boston, in 1870, an English Bulldog was crossed with a white English Terrier, and from this mating came all Boston Terriers, previously called Round Heads or Bull Terriers. There was probably considerable inbreeding and some French Bulldog blood mixed in before the breed was standardized.

Aptitude: A descendent of parents long established as bull baiters, the Boston was bred and remains with but one purpose, that of a family pet, a companion.

Size: This breed is divided into three classes: under 15 pounds (6.8 kg); 15 pounds and under 20 pounds (9 kg); 20 pounds and not more than 25 pounds (11.3 kg).

Coat: The Boston's fine coat must be short, smooth, bright, and shiny.

Colors: Brindle, seal, or black colors are allowed, all marked with white in specified patterns. Solid colors are disqualified.

Coat care and exercise: A short-bristle brush, rubber currycomb, or grooming mitt is used to remove dead coat and bring out a shine to the Boston's coat.

Exercise is not a major consideration of this companion animal. Although it loves to play, it has no use for long walks, and insists on accompanying its owners everywhere.

Attitude: The clever Boston has a well-developed sense of humor. It is a loyal, playful, affectionate pet that rarely barks except as a warning. Enthusiastic, fun-loving, and self-confident, this dog gets along well with other pets and especially with children.

Training: The Boston Terrier needs training just as any other breed does. It is a biddable, intelligent little dog that is not difficult to teach. Highly sensitive to voice intonations, it learns its lessons quickly and without nagging or badgering. Be sure to intersperse training with play.

Bichon Frisé

Origin: Correct pronunciation of this dog's strange name is *Bee-shahn-Free-zay*, which means curly-haired puppy. Its precise origin among the Mediterranean countries is unknown, but was probably in Belgium or France. *Bichon* is shortened from *Barbichon*, named for its ancestor, the Barbet or Water Spaniel. It is also called the Tenerife Dog and is one of four Bichon breeds with common Mediterranean origins.

Aptitude: Once a favorite of kings and courtiers of Europe, the Bichon has at various times sunk to the level of street dog, circus dog, and organ grinder's dog. It has one particular aptitude—that of making its family quite happy.

Size: Bichons stand 9 inches (22.8 cm) to 12 inches (30.5 cm) tall.

Coat: This breed sports a unique covering. Its coat is double, with a soft and dense undercoat and outer hair of a coarser and curlier texture.

Bichon Frisé.

It feels like deep, plush velvet and springs back when patted down.

Colors: The Bichon is solid white, without markings. Slight shading of buff, cream, or apricot is sometimes seen on the ears.

Coat care and exercise: The drawback to owning a Bichon is its grooming needs. Its luxurious coat requires daily combing and occasional clipping. Regular washing is required to maintain its snowy white color.

Offsetting its grooming requirements, this little dog's exercise needs are met by running around the house or apartment.

Attitude: Further offsetting its extensive grooming needs is the Bichon's beautiful character and temperament. It bonds very tightly with its owner and is an admirable companion. Intelligent, pliable, cheerful, and active, this dog is content to be a family member, accompanying its humans everywhere. It accepts other pets easily and is great with children.

Training: This dog accepts training in stride, is bright and clever, and learns quickly. The Bichon's former role as circus performer is evident in its ready acceptance of training. It is sensitive to voice modulations, and eager to please.

Lhasa Apso

Origin: Although its origin is clouded, we know that about 13 centuries ago, in Tibetan monasteries, the Lhasa Apso served as a chamber guard. The two parts of the breed name have widely different meanings. *Lhasa* probably refers to the capital of Tibet. *Apso* refers to *goatlike* and is associated with the flowing coarse coat that might be thought of as being like the beard of a goat. Its native name is *Abso Seng Kye*, which translates to Bark Lion Sentinel Dog.

Aptitude: Originally quite intertwined with Buddhist beliefs related to reincarnation, the Lhasa is now a fine family pet, great show dog, and admirable watchdog.

Size: The size is variable, but usually between 10 and 11 inches (25 to 27 cm) tall for males, and slightly smaller for females.

Coat: Lhasa coats are heavy, straight, hard, and dense. They are not wooly or silky.

Colors: Virtually all colors are permissible.

Coat care and exercise: No less than weekly grooming is needed with comb and brush. To dress this dog for showing requires even more attention to its coat, which is the reason many pet owners elect to trim Lhasas with scissors and clippers.

Exercise needs for the Lhasa are moderate. It can derive most of its exercise running about in its normal daily activities. Long walks are appreciated, but not necessary.

Attitude: Usually thought of as a lapdog, the Lhasa Apso is calm, loyal, and cheerful. It is also independent, and although it likes company, it won't cling to its owner. It is a lovable little dog that socializes well with other house pets. It makes a great playmate and friend for children, but is rather withdrawn or cautious of strangers.

Training: This breed has the reputation of inflexibility. It requires ample rewards for its correct performance, and will become moody and

Lhasa Apso.

obstinate if nagged or overcorrected. Teaching tricks or other more sophisticated performances will be difficult. Patience and consistency are required, but normal obedience training is possible and housebreaking is almost automatic.

Chow Chow

Origin: The origin of this breed is lost in antiquity. It is said to have existed as a breed in the Han dynasty about 150 B.C. in China and may have come from the arctic regions. It is one of the oldest breeds in existence and probably is of Spitz origin, or conversely, may be a progenitor of some of the Spitz-type breeds of today. Known also as the Black Tongue Dog, Wolf Dog, and Bear Dog, the Chow Chow has been immensely popular in China for centuries. The breed's interesting name is said to come from a pidgin English term for miscellaneous articles brought from the Orient and refers to knickknacks or bric-a-brac.

Aptitude: The Chow's background is speckled with many uses. Its meat was served as a delicacy on the table of emperors; its hide was worn for warmth. It was an adept hunting dog, guard dog, sled dog, and all-around family pet. Today, the Chow is primarily a companion with strong watchdog tendencies.

Size: Dogs and bitches usually weigh about 45 to 70 pounds (20 to 32 kg) and stand 17 to 20 inches (43 to 50 cm) tall.

Coat: The Chow Chow has two coat types: rough and smooth. Both coats are double. The rough coat is covered with guard hair that is abundant, dense, straight and coarse, and off-standing. The undercoat is soft, thick, and wooly. The smooth-coated Chow's coat is similar in every way but the quantity and distribution and character of the outer hair.

Colors: Five colors are permissible: red, black, blue, cinnamon, and cream. All are judged together and equally.

Coat care and exercise: Although the smooth-coated dogs have less grooming requirements, all Chow Chows need regular attention with comb and brush.

Exercise needs are moderate for this large, muscular dog, but it thrives on outside living in a cool environment. In cooler weather, the Chow enjoys long walks and romps in the park.

Attitude: This dog has a mind of its own. Lordly in action, even its walk

Chow Chow.

is dignified and stately. It is suspicious of strangers, and a fine watchdog. Not terribly affectionate, the Chow is sometimes stubborn, but peaceful and calm. It is a dominant dog and is often assertive toward others of its kind. Usually not considered a child's playmate, some Chows become quite attached to older children.

Training: This dog needs an experienced, understanding, and authoritative trainer who is consistent in approach; it won't tolerate bullying.

Chinese Shar-Pei

Origin: As you might have guessed, this breed comes from China. It probably shares lineage with the Chow Chow, both having black tongues and originating in the same dynasty. It was once a menu item, a herd guard dog for sheep, and it was specially bred for pit fighting. *Shar-Pei* is translated as *sand skin*, or sandpaperlike coat.

Aptitude: Today's Shar-Pei population serves as a companion dog. It is a unique-appearing pet, once touted as a rare breed, bordering on extinction.

Size: Both males and bitches weigh 40 to 55 pounds (18 to 25 kg) and stand 18 to 20 inches (45 to 51 cm) tall. The female is slightly smaller than the male.

Coat: The extremely harsh coat stands stiff and straight from this dog's body.

Colors: Any solid color is acceptable.

Coat care and exercise: The Shar-Pei's coat requires very little brushing, but its wrinkled skin needs regular attention. Its multiple folds of skin may become irritated and infected, and should be inspected daily.

Exercise is quite important for this breed, and regular outdoor walks and games are important to keep the dog happy and healthy.

Attitude: The Shar-Pei is a dominant breed that displays loyalty to its owner. It is a brave, playful, and active dog that has a mind of its own. It bonds well with its family, but is suspicious of strangers. Since it has a heritage in the fighting pit, introducing it to other dogs must be done cautiously.

Training: Training is best accomplished by experienced people who understand the breed. Confidence,

Chinese Shar-Pei.

authority, and consistency are important when training the Shar-Pei; an uncertain trainer will soon find the student-teacher roles reversed.

Herding Group

German Shepherd Dog
Origin: Old herding breeds were combined to produce the German Shepherd Dog in the late 1800s in Germany, although an early writer traced its origin back to the Bronze Age. Its progenitors include the German Hovawart and numerous farm-herding dogs.

Aptitude: Bred originally as a herd dog, this dog has excelled at nearly every task known to dogdom. It has been used as a war dog, guide dog, handicap dog, police assistant, drug sniffer, search-and-rescue dog, sentry dog, guard dog, and more. Its most important aptitude is probably companion dog.

Size: Males stand 24 to 26 inches (61 to 66 cm) tall, and bitches stand 22 to 24 inches (52 to 61 cm) tall.

Coat: According to the breed standard, the coat is double and of medium length. The guard coat is quite dense, and is made up of straight, harsh hair that lies close.

Colors: Various colors are permissible, but white dogs are disqualified.

Coat care and exercise: Combing and brushing regularly will help to keep this dog's dense coat and your furniture looking good.

German Shepherd Dog.

A bored Shepherd is often found engaged in mischief. Although it is a great companion dog, the exercise requirements of an athletic and energetic dog can't be neglected. Regular long walks, runs in the park, and dog sports are the best means of exercising the German Shepherd Dog.

Attitude: Intelligence and an eagerness to please are the Shepherd's greatest attributes. This dog is friendly, if slightly reserved toward strangers. It is active, alert, brave, and above all, loyal to its family. Correct introduction to other pets should be accomplished early in the Shepherd's life. The Shepherd is wonderfully protective and appreciative of children of the family, and will accept friends if appropriately introduced. The Shepherd, like other herding breeds, is not usually predisposed to wander or run away.

Training: One of the most trainable of all dogs, the Shepherd thrives on any type of training. They have become accomplished trackers, herders, rescue dogs, and obedience dogs. Frisbee, agility contests, fly ball, and other dog sports are taken in stride. The training possibilities are nearly endless, and the more you can challenge a German Shepherd Dog, the happier it will be.

Shetland Sheepdog

Origin: This herding dog was bred from the same stock that produced our modern Collie in the Shetland Islands, Scotland. Collies and Shetlands developed at roughly the same time, and for a time the breed was called the Shetland Collie.

Aptitude: A breed adept at herding sheep and other farm animals, the Sheltie has carved out a place as a wonderful family pet as well. Shetland Sheepdogs also are often winners in obedience, agility trials, and Frisbee contests.

Size: Shelties stand 13 to 16 inches (33 to 40 cm) tall.

Coat: The guard hairs of the Sheltie's double coat are long, straight, and harsh; the undercoat is short and furry.

Colors: Colors permissible are black, blue merle, and sable. All are marked with varying amounts of white and/or tan.

Coat care and exercise: Comb and brush grooming should be done weekly and more often during shedding.

Never forget that this is a busy, workaholic, herding dog that needs exercise to prevent boredom. Although the Sheltie adapts to backyard exercise, it has great stamina and strength and enjoys long walks and a more challenging and active life.

Attitude: A Sheltie's intelligence is among its greatest attributes. This clever dog is loyal to its master, obedient, affectionate, and responsive. It is extremely sociable and accepts other small pets and other dogs. Usually cautious of strangers, this dog is a gentle and playful child's pet that isn't apt to wander away.

Training: Having an untrained Sheltie is like owning an expensive sports car and leaving it in the garage. This dog thrives on training. It is a biddable animal, easy to train, and eager to please. Sensitive to voice modulations, it trains without nagging. Shelties are great candi-

Shetland Sheepdog.

dates for agility trials, obedience work, and other dog sports.

Collie

Origin: The origin of the Collie dates back into Scottish and English history for centuries. Originally called the Scotch Collie, it was apparently bred about the same time and in similar regions of Scotland as the Shetland Sheepdog. For the last two centuries, the smooth and rough Collie varieties were working herd dogs, and no pedigrees were kept.

Aptitude: Bred for hundreds of years to herd livestock, this dog has been relocated to herd children. Its principal vocation today is that of family pet, companion dog, and show dog.

Size: Males weigh 60 to 75 pounds (27 to 34 kg) and stand 24 to 26 inches (61 to 66 cm) tall. Females weigh 50 to 65 pounds (23 to 30 kg) and stand 22 to 24 inches (56 to 61 cm) tall.

Coat: The rough Collie's guard coat is straight and harsh; the undercoat is soft, furry, and dense. The smooth Collie has a short, hard, dense, flat single coat.

Colors: Collies are shown in four colors: sable and white, tricolor, blue merle, and white.

Coat care and exercise: The rough Collie needs extensive grooming; comb and brush should be applied several times weekly. The smooth Collie requires much less coat attention, and weekly grooming with a rubber currycomb or stiff brush should suffice.

The Collie does best with an abundance of exercise, but is adaptable to a more sedentary life, if necessary. It will make the most of runs in the park, walks in the woods, or dog sports.

Attitude: The Collie is quite intelligent, eager to please, clever, and energetic. It is lovable, sensitive, and affectionate. It bonds closely with its family, and usually has no tendency to wander away from home.

The Collie accepts other dogs quite well and is great with children. Stories have been told of Collies that herd their small children and keep them at home without the benefit of fences. Not known as a great watchdog, it nevertheless tends to be vigilant and cautious around strangers.

Training: Training a Collie is an easy job. It is a quick learner that seems to understand your commands rapidly. There is no need to

Collie.

nag or scold the Collie; it will respond better to a gentle voice and handling. The Collie has proven itself to be an easy study for agility trials, obedience training, fly ball, and herding trials.

Welsh Corgi, Pembroke

Origin: Tracing its origin to the twelfth century, the Welsh Corgi, Pembroke, is the progeny of dogs that were brought to Wales by Flemish weavers. These dogs are described as similar to Schipperkes and came from the same family that produced Keeshonds, Pomeranians, Samoyeds, and Chow Chows. It later developed in Pembrokeshire to its present state.

Aptitude: For years, the Corgi was a farm dog with natural herding instincts, but today the Pembroke is better known as an agreeable family pet.

Size: Males weigh 30 pounds (13 kg) or slightly less, and bitches weigh 28 pounds (12 kg). Both male

Pembroke Welsh Corgi.

and female should stand 10 to 12 inches (25 to 30 cm) tall.

Coat: The Pembroke Corgi's coat is double; the undercoat is medium length, short, and thick with guard hair that is longer and coarser.

Colors: Self colors of red, sable, fawn, and black and tan, with or without white markings, are permissible in the Pembroke.

Coat care and exercise: Grooming the Corgi coat is easy, although weekly brushing and combing shedding hair or mats is required.

Exercise requirements for this short-legged dog are significant. It loves dog sports and yard balls, but it also needs extensive leash exercise or romps with its children.

Attitude: The Corgi is an energetic, hardy, and intelligent herding dog. Even-tempered and lovable, the dog will wrestle and play all day with children, but doesn't appreciate teasing. It is alert but not overly suspicious of strangers. It usually accepts other dogs, but is somewhat dominant to its own kind.

Training: The Corgi responds well to training and usually catches on quickly. It can be taught tricks and often does well in agility and obedience trials. This dog is very biddable but should be trained with consistency.

Australian Shepherd

Origin: Naturally, Australian Shepherds originated in Australia, right? Wrong. This breed traces its ancestry to the Basque region of France and Spain and is probably related to other herding dogs of Europe. When Basque herdsmen immigrated first to Australia, then to the western United States, they took their sheep and dogs with them. Through various crosses and careful selection, the Australian Shepherd emerged, the product of American animal husbandry.

Aptitude: The Aussie remains a popular dog on working ranches in the West, and is often seen trailing alongside cowboys' horses or riding on top of loads of hay being moved down the road. However, with more Shepherds than sheep, this dog has naturally found its secondary niche in city and country homes.

Size: Males stand 20 to 23 inches (53 to 55 cm) tall, and bitches, 18 to 21 inches (46 to 52 cm) tall.

Coat: Aussies have a double coat, the guard hair of which is of medium texture, straight to wavy, and the undercoat development depends on the climate and weather conditions.

Colors: Aussies are blue merle, black, red merle, red, all with or without white markings and tan or copper points.

Coat care and exercise: Relatively little care is needed for this outdoor dog's coat. Combing is occasionally required to remove mats or to assist in seasonal shedding.

Exercise is a major consideration for Australian Shepherd owners. If not on a livestock ranch, owners should think of dog sports of any type. A bored Aussie is bound to turn to mischief to occupy itself.

Australian Shepherd.

Attitude: This relatively new breed is intelligent, eager to please, active, and tough. It is extremely loyal to its owners, and has stamina to burn. It is a good watchdog, and being a herding dog, gets along well with other animals. Aussies are usually good with children but may be shy around strangers and visitors. In the case of working dogs, the Aussie is considered a one-man dog.

Training: The close bonding between handler and dog is obvious when the Australian is in training. Eager and quick to learn, the dog seems to read the handler's mind. This breed needs to be kept busy, and is a wonderful candidate for agility trials, Frisbee and fly ball contests, and obedience. Herding trials are wonderful sports for this dog, if available.

Old English Sheepdog

Origin: From its name you might guess the origin of this breed is

Old English Sheepdog.

England. The evidence shows the Old English Sheepdog was developed in the counties of Devon and Somerset. It may have Scottish Bearded Collie or Russian Owtchar dogs in its background.

Aptitude: Retaining its drover's instincts, the Old English is today kept more for companionship and showing than work.

Size: The standard lists no weight limits, but males stand 22 inches (55.8 cm), and females stand 21 inches (53.3 cm) tall.

Coat: The Sheepdog has a profuse coat that is hard, not straight, but shaggy and free from curl.

Colors: Any shade of gray, grizzle, blue, or blue merle, with or without white markings, or in reverse, are permissible.

Coat care and exercise: This breed enjoys rather intensive coat care. It should be combed and brushed three or four times weekly to maintain the coat in show condition and free of mats and tangles. More work on the shaggy coat is needed during shedding seasons. Non-show owners may elect to groom with scissors and clippers instead.

The Old English Sheepdog needs regular exercise, although it isn't as demanding as some breeds. Playing ball with it, or entering it in dog sports will aid in providing ample exercise.

Attitude: An intelligent dog, the Old English is quite amiable, adaptable to various lifestyles, and very social. It adores its family and is a great playmate for children. Not considered to be an alert or vigilant watchdog, it accepts other dogs and strangers with very brief introductions.

Training: Eager to please and easily trained, this dog rarely exhibits dominant behavior. Gentle consistency is the most important factor for training.

Australian Cattle Dog

Origin: Developed in Australia, the Australian Cattle Dog has ancestors that include the wild but silent Australian Dingo, Blue Merle Collie, Dalmatian, and the Black and Tan Kelpie. This dog was fromerly known as the Queensland Blue Heeler.

Aptitude: The Australian Cattle Dog is primarily a herding dog, and excels in that work. It has recently become more of an all-around pet in the United States, and now is considered a better than average companion for active, rural residents.

Size: Males stand 18 to 20 inches (46 to 51 cm) tall. Females stand 17 to 29 inches (43 to 48 cm) tall.

Coat: A short, dense undercoat is covered with straight, medium-length and -texture, weather-resistant guard hair.

Colors: The Australian Cattle Dog can be either red speckle or blue. The blue dogs have blue or blue-mottled coats with or without other markings on the head. The red speckle is an evenly distributed speckle over the entire body, and darker red head markings are preferable.

Coat care and exercise: The coat of this dog requires very little attention; occasional grooming with comb and brush is sufficient.

A working breed like the Australian needs an abundance of exercise and work to keep it content. This dog's mental and physical condition depends on regular exercise.

Attitude: This breed, like most other herding dogs, is quite intelligent and willing to share in your work. It is loyal, hardy, and active. It behaves well around children, and is an active participant in their activi-

Australian Cattle Dog.

ties. The Australian Cattle Dog readily accepts other dogs and is usually ready for most dog sports.

Training: Whether using this dog in its primary capacity as a herd dog or as a companion, its training should begin early. It is active and eager to please, and training should be easy, but it appreciates daily work or training, and becomes bored and moody if neglected. Agility training, fly ball, obedience work, and Frisbee are right up this dog's alley.

Glossary

Agility trial: Timed sporting event in which dogs must master a group of obstacles laid out in a course.

Alpha dog: Leader of the pack; chief dog.

Aptitude: Natural ability or talent; general suitability.

Associative learning: Method of teaching a dog by linking an act to a reward.

Backyard breeder: Amateur or hobby producer of dogs, not necessarily interested in improving the breed.

Biddable: Cooperative, willing to obey the handler.

Bite: Position of dog's incisor teeth when the mouth is closed.

Body language: Physical attitude of a dog that tells the handler what action the dog is considering.

Bond: Invisible reciprocal attachment between a dog and its master.

Bumper: A stuffed canvas retrieving toy that resembles a boat fender.

Canis familiaris: Genus and species of the domestic dog.

Carnivore: An animal that subsists primarily on animal flesh.

Champion: A dog that has competed in AKC shows or trials and has earned sufficient points to be awarded the Champion title.

CHD: Canine Hip Dysplasia; a hereditary deformity of the femur and pelvis.

Check cord or check line: Long, lightweight line attached to the dog's collar to enable the handler to control the dog from a distance.

Choke collar: Chain or nylon check collar used for training.

Cognitive ability: Capacity to understand or absorb knowledge.

Conformation: Form and structure of a dog compared to the breed standard.

Congenital disease: Deformity present at birth, not necessarily hereditary.

Corded: A coat allowed to grow naturally, into long, uncombed dreadlocks or ropelike cords.

Cryptorchid: A dog with both testicles retained in the abdominal cavity.

Dead ring: On a training collar, the ring through which the chain is dropped to form a noose.

Dependence: Trust in and reliance of a dog on its handler.

Direct negative reinforcement: Physical correction of a dog using a personal disciplinary measure such as scolding or hitting.

Discipline: 1. Training in a specific endeavor. 2. Chastisement or punishment. 3. Control.

DNA: Deoxyribonucleic acid, a molecular basis of heredity, located in tissue cells' nuclei.

Dog show: Judged canine exhibition used to compare registered dogs to the breed standard and to each other.

Dominance training: Activities owners use to establish themselves as dominant members of a dog's pack.

Elbow dysplasia: Un-united anconeal process; hereditary, developmental deformity of the elbow joint.

Fecal exam: Microscopic examination of feces for evidence of parasite ova.

Feral: Wild; undomesticated, or having escaped from domestication.

Fetch: Game in which the handler throws an article that is recovered and returned by the dog.

Fly ball: A box with a treadle that the dog steps on to cause a ball to pop out, and the dog must catch and return to handler.

Focus: Concentration of the dog upon its handler.

Force: To physically cause a dog to do something beyond its natural inclination. Restraint and dominance training are types of force. Force does not imply abuse.

Frisbee: 1. A plastic disk manufactured for throwing and catching. 2. A judged canine competition using disks.

Gene pool: Collection of genes of all the dogs in the breeding population.

Habituation: Training by becoming accustomed or conditioned to a given incident or situation.

Heartworm: Bloodstream parasite of dogs, spread by mosquitoes.

Hereditary: Genetically transmitted.

Hyperactive: Describing a dog that displays excessive activity with attention deficit.

Imprinting: Rapid learning process that takes place early in the life of a social animal and establishes a behavior pattern.

Innate: Inherent; natural; describing factors that are present from birth.

Instinct: A natural or inherent aptitude.

Intelligence: The ability to learn, understand, and solve problems through reasoning.

Mismarked: Describing a coat with markings that are undesirable for conformation showing.

Monorchid: Having one testicle retained in abdominal cavity.

Mouthing: Normal action of a puppy investigating its environment by tasting.

Negative reinforcement: Dissuading a dog from repeating an incorrect response to training by scolding or physically correcting the behavior.

Neophobia: Fear of new things; the dominant characteristic of feral animals that is undesirable in training prospects.

Neoteny: Immature characteristics retained in adulthood.

Nest etiquette: Manners governing young puppies' actions in the presence of dam and siblings.

Obedience: Discipline involving modification of many different behaviors through extensive training.

OFA: Orthopedic Foundation for Animals, the organization that reads and evaluates X rays for hereditary diseases.

Olfactory sense: Ability to smell and differentiate odors.

Olfactory system: Organs and tissues associated with smell.

Overshot: Upper incisors that protrude over the lowers.

Pack mentality: Innate wolflike instinct of a dog to be loyal to the pack leader, either canine or human.

Pedigree: Genealogical chart of a dog showing a few generations of ancestors.

Pet quality: Describing a purebred dog that has features that make it undesirable for conformation showing or breeding.

Plucking: To remove a dog's dead coat by hand and thin its coat a few hairs at a time.

Positive reinforcement: Any reward for proper performance.

Progenitor: Ancestor or parent.

Progeny: Offspring or descendants.

Prong collar. Restraint device using a series of blunt prongs that turn into the dog's neck when tightened.

Punishment: Physical negative reinforcement of a command.

Puppy mill or puppy factory: Dog-breeding establishment that places quantity above quality of the puppies produced.

Release: The final phase of training a specific task; command that returns the dog to its normal status.

Remote reinforcement: Use of a separated or distant tool to assist in training, such as a squirt bottle, a long line, noise, and so on.

Retracting lead: Long leash contained within a spring-loaded handle that can be drawn in quickly.

Reward: Any recognized appreciation given to the dog being trained.

Selective breeding: Scientific mating to encourage or produce specific characteristics in the offspring.

Show quality: Describing registered dogs that have excellent conformation, color, and movement according to the breed standard.

Siblings: Littermates; brothers and sisters.

Skijoring: Sport in which a team of one, two, or three dogs pulls the handler who is standing on skis.

Socialization: Process of adapting to a human environment.

Submissive or subservient attitude: Combination of postures taken by a puppy when meeting other dogs.

Temperament: Personality; mental attitude or character of a dog.

Tidbits: Physical rewards or food.

Toilet area: A designated spot in the yard where a dog goes to defecate and urinate.

Trainability: Dog's ability and desire to learn; propensity of a dog to focus on its handler and accept direction.

Training ring: Ring on a training collar to which the leash is snapped.

Umbilical hernia: Congenital outpouching of abdominal tissues resulting from a lack of fusion of the muscles.

Undershot: Lower incisors protruding beyond the uppers.

Work-play balance: Essential part of any training that refers to the need to intermingle training with play.

Worm check: Fecal examination to determine endoparasite infestation.

Yard ball: Hollow, firm plastic ball that is too large for the dog to pick up, yet small enough for the dog to toss it around by using the top of its muzzle and its feet.

Useful Addresses and Literature

Associations

American Boarding Kennel Association
4575 Galley Road, Suite 400-A
Colorado Springs, CO 80915

American Humane Association
9725 East Hampton Avenue
Denver, CO 80231

American Kennel Club
260 Madison Avenue
New York, NY 10016
Web site: http://www.AKC.org
For Registration, Records, Litter
   Information:
5580 Centerview Drive
Raleigh, NC 27606

American Veterinary Medical Association
930 North Meacham Road
Schaumburg, IL 60173

Canadian Kennel Club
111 Eglington Avenue
Toronto 12, Ontario
Canada

Canine Eye Registry Foundation (CERF)
South Campus Court, Building C
West Lafayette, IN 47907

Institute for Genetic Disease Control
   (GDC)
P.O. Box 222
Davis, CA 95617

Kennel Club, The
1-4 Clargis Street
Picadilly
London W7Y8AB
England

Morris Animal Foundation
45 Inverness Drive East
Englewood, CO 80112-5480

National Dog Registry (tattoo, microchip)
P.O. Box 116
Woodstock, NY 12498

Orthopedic Foundation for Animals
   (OFA)
2300 Nifong Boulevard
Columbia, MO 65201

Owner-Handler Association of America
583 Knoll Court
Seaford, NY 11783

Tattoo-A-Pet
Department 1625
Emmons Avenue
Brooklyn, NY 11235

Periodicals

AKC Gazette
51 Madison Avenue
New York, NY 10010

Dog Fancy Magazine
P.O. Box 53264
Boulder, CO 80322-3264

Dog World
29 North Wacker Drive
Chicago, IL 60606

Gaines Touring with Towser
P.O. Box 5700
Kankakee, IL 60902

Books

Alderton, David. *Dogs*. New York: DK Publishing Company, 1993.

American Animal Hospital Association. *Encyclopedia of Dog Health and Care*. New York: The Philip Lief Group, Inc., 1994

American Kennel Club. *The Complete Dog Book*. New York: Macmillan Publishing Co., 1992.

Animal Medical Center. *The Complete Book of Dog Health*. New York: Howell Book House, 1985.

Clark, Ross D., and Joan R. Stainer. *Medical and Genetic Aspects of Purebred Dogs*. Fairway, Kansas, and St. Simons Island, Georgia: Forum Publications, Inc., 1994.

Coile, Caroline D. *Encyclopedia of Dog Breeds*. Hauppauge, New York: Barron's Educational Series, Inc., 1998.

Davis, Henry P. *The Modern Dog Encyclopedia*. Harrisburg, Pennsylvania: The Stackpole Company, 1958.

Lorenz, Michael D., and Larry M. Cornelius. *Small Animal Medical Diagnosis*. Philadelphia, Pennsylvania: J.B. Lippincott Company, 1993.

Verhoef-Verhallen, Esther. *Encyclopaedia of Dogs*. Lisse, The Netherlands: Rebo Productions, 1996.

Waters, B. *Fetch and Carry*. Printed in 1894 by B. Waters.

Yamazaki, Tetsu. *Legacy of the Dog*. San Francisco, California: Chronicle Books, 1995.

Index